Alwyn Thomson is Research Officer with ECONI. He is the editor of two earlier books published by ECONI as part of this project: *Faith in Ulster* (1996) and *The Great White Tent* (1999).

FIELDS OF VISION

Faith and Identity
in Protestant Ireland

Alwyn Thomson

Centre for Contemporary Christianity in Ireland
A Ministry of ECONI

Published by: Centre for Contemporary Christianity in Ireland
Howard House
1 Bunswick Street
Belfast
BT2 7GE

The Centre for Contemporary Christianity in Ireland
is a ministry of ECONI

Cover design by: Spring Graphics

Printed by: Dataplus

This book has received support from the Cultural Diversity Programme of the Community Relations Council, which aims to encourage acceptance and understanding of cultural diversity. The views expressed do not necessarily reflect those of the NI Community Relations Council.

This project has been supported by the Joseph Rowntree Charitable Trust.

ISBN 1 874324 56 5
© ECONI 2002

CONTENTS

Foreword   1

Introduction   3

Part 1

1 God Who Made Thee Mighty:
   The Shaping of Protestant England   9

2 A Fearful People:
   Protestant Ireland in the Nineteenth Century   31

3 Keeping the Faith:
   Religion and the Troubles   55

Part 2

4 Everything Looks Different:
   Self, Society and the Triune God   73

5 This Other Eden:
   Identity, Belonging and Place   97

6 Trinity, Church, Kingdom:
   The Community of God in Northern Ireland   125

Notes   141

Bibliography   149

FOREWORD

The call to follow Jesus is never heard in a vacuum. It comes to each of us who hear it in the context of our lives as part of a community, living in a particular place and at a specific point in history. Over the centuries Christians have sought to interpret their calling in this matrix of belonging, which bonds us to our people, our place and our time.

If, as Paul reminds us, we struggle as individuals on the journey of faith against the allure of the world, the flesh and the devil, it has often been our failure to discern the potency of its communal manifestation that has done most to undermine our faithfulness. For it has been the heady brew of God, land and nation that has most threatened our witness as faith communities.

At the heart of following Jesus is the question of identity. 'Jesus is LORD' is not simply the earliest confession of a follower, but it defines who that person is in relation to the state, the tribe, other worldviews and religions, and the very world and created order itself. This is the new beginning, the conversion, that being born again, which requires a new understanding of who we are in relation to our people, our place and our time.

While many Christians in Northern Ireland are well taught on what that may mean in personal terms, we struggle to bring the same radical renewal of our being to the realm of communal identity. Our long history of conflict bears witness to the failure of the church throughout Europe and across many centuries to allow this gospel call to create a new humanity across the boundaries of culture and politics. Instead we have persevered with the besetting sin of Christendom and created God in our image - we are the people, this is the place and God is on our side.

Since its inception in 1987 ECONI has been concerned with how biblical conversion looks and is experienced in the context of a long-standing identity conflict, with its communal hate and violence. Fifteen years later the commitment to bring religious nationalism, whether in its Irish nationalist or Ulster unionist guises, to the test of biblical values has more than a local significance. Eastern Europe, East Africa, and the growing polarisation between the west and the Islamic world put these issues at the heart of the world stage.

In this book Alwyn Thomson sets the issues in our 'wee place', within our social, political and religious history. It tells a story of Protestant identity in Ireland, with its strengths and failures. Most importantly it brings us back to Jesus, marking not so much the end of a project as a refreshing well on our journey to be the people of God in this place for this time. As such it is something that all followers of Jesus need to do in their own place if they are to be careful in being true to their life in Christ.

David W Porter

Lent 2002

INTRODUCTION

WITHOUT A VISION THE PEOPLE PERISH

All of us need a vision. We need a vision of the past that tells us where we have come from and who we are – "the rock whence we are hewn". We also need a vision for the future that can inspire motivate and sustain us through life. Yet all of our visions – of the past or of the future – are flawed and insufficient. "We see through a glass darkly" in more areas of life than we care to acknowledge.

And so we stand in the constantly shifting space between our vision of the past and our vision of the future, and in the ambiguous space between our need for that vision without which we will perish and the truth that our vision is seen only through darkness.

A shifting space, an ambiguous space is, inevitably, a potentially threatening space. Surely it is not only a vision that we need, but an unwavering vision – one that makes sense of our past and offers us a sure and steadfast hope for the future. However, that need for an unwavering vision demands that we find solid ground on which to stand. That solid ground, in turn, determines our field of vision – and its limitations.

Yet one of the greatest gifts we have as human beings is the ability to step off the solid ground, to see the world – our past or our future – from a different point of view, to shift our field of vision. And what is true of men and women in general is surely true of Christians in particular, for, when we step off the solid ground of our human perspective, we continue to stand on the solid rock that is Christ.

Changing our field of vision can have two consequences. We can find a new vision that enlightens, a vision that changes our understanding.

But more than that we can find a new vision that transforms, a vision that not only changes how we think but how we live.

VISION AND UNDERSTANDING

The aim of the first part of this book is to change our field of vision in order to create a fuller understanding of the identity of Irish Protestantism. Specifically, it aims to deepen understanding in three areas:

1. The extent to which British identity has been shaped by Protestantism,

2. The extent to which Irish unionism was a local manifestation of that British Protestant identity, and

3. The extent to which Protestantism remains a core aspect of unionist identity.

Chapter 1 surveys the relationship between Protestantism and English - and, by extension, British - identity from the time of the English Reformation to the Victorian era. The chapter argues that Protestantism was a crucial component in the development of English and British identity. Chapter 2 looks at the Protestant community in Ireland in the nineteenth and early twentieth centuries against a backdrop of the growing power and confidence of the Catholic church and the rise of Irish nationalism. It argues that this British community in Ireland shared the Protestant identity of Britain and that this played a significant role in shaping the nature of Protestant reaction to Catholicism and nationalism.

Chapters 1 and 2 taken together aim to demonstrate the truth of Michael Ignatieff's assertion that "a visit to Ulster is to travel down through the layers of historical time that separate mainland Britain from a Britishness that was once its own." The Protestantism of the British in Ireland is seen to be a reflection of the Protestantism that has been at the heart of British identity since the sixteenth century and has only ceased to be of importance in the latter part of the twentieth century.

Chapter 3 asks to what extent religion - in particular, conservative Protestant religion - is still a factor in shaping the attitudes and values of the Protestant community in Northern Ireland. It analyses and criticises a number of key works which minimise the importance of religion and a number which stress the importance of religion, concluding that the former are deeply flawed by virtue of the inability of their authors to understand the nature of religious belief and, consequently, its continuing relevance to the situation. The chapter also aims to demonstrate the continuing relevance of religion with reference to the role of conservative Protestant religion during the referendum on the Belfast Agreement in1998.

VISION AND TRANSFORMATION

Understanding is important, but a new understanding is only the beginning. "Son of man," says the God of Israel to the prophet Ezekiel, "what is this proverb you have in the land of Israel: 'The days go by and every vision comes to nothing'? Say to them, 'This is what the Sovereign LORD says: I am going to put an end to this proverb, and they will no longer quote it in Israel.' Say to them, 'The days are near when every vision will be fulfilled.'" The power of visions lies in their ability to transform us and, through us, to transform our society.

The aim of the second part of this book is to continue to search for a deeper understanding, but focusing less on our historical past than on our theological past. Specifically it aims to deepen understanding in three areas:

1. The vision of God, land and nation common among Protestants in Northern Ireland,

2. The vision of God, land and nation made known in the Bible, and

3. The power of these biblical visions to transform and renew our vision.

Chapter 4 looks at the relationship between visions of God and social and political visions, arguing that the two are closely related. The chapter provides a description of this relationship in the religious and political thinking of conservative Protestants in Northern Ireland. While accepting the legitimacy of the vision of God common within conservative Protestantism it argues that other visions of God could provide a more coherent and fuller perspective. In particular, in focuses on a trinitarian vision of God and a corresponding theological anthropology as having the potential to reconfigure social and political thinking.

Chapter 5 addresses the twin themes of land and nation, belonging and identity. It looks at biblical models from both Old and New Testaments arguing that the human need for belonging and identity is God given, but is also transcended and transformed in the light of the New Testament's emphasis on kingdom and church.

Chapter 6 summarises the biblical perspective and sets out the challenge of living with the tension between belonging and identity as gift and belonging and identity as temptation. It elucidates the relationship between Trinity, kingdom and church and suggests that it is vital to incorporate this thinking into the church's teaching, preaching and liturgy, for it is only when the church learns what it means to be the church that it is in a position to make any wider impact on society.

It is, finally, in the life of the church that transformation has to start. As Northern Ireland faces times of change, as we together reassess our past and contemplate our future, will the church be up to the challenge of recognising, expressing and living out the transforming vision of the Bible for the good of the church, the benefit of society and the glory of God?

I would like to thank the Joseph Rowntree Charitable Trust who have supported the project since its inception; the Community Relations Council who have supported the publication of this book; and Megan Halteman and Amy Ornee who proofread the text.

PART 1

1

GOD WHO MADE THEE MIGHTY

The Shaping of Protestant England

GLORIANA

England under the Tudors[1]

The Protestant Reformation that Henry Tudor initiated was a half-hearted affair in matters of religion. Henry's primary purpose was to break the power of the Roman Catholic Church and to evince the loyalty of the people. Henry's skilful propaganda, designed to produce religious antipathy towards Catholicism and national antipathy towards Spain, Europe's leading Catholic power, ensured that the ground was prepared beforehand and, as a result, there was little resistance to his actions.

Henry's death brought his nine year old son Edward to the throne. The king and his chief advisors shared a strong commitment to the cause of Protestantism, and these years were marked by a more consistently Protestant policy. His reign saw the publication of the Forty-Two Articles, setting out the doctrinal position of the English Church, and the Book of Common Prayer. Both reflected an increasingly Protestant theology and church order. Yet, despite the increasing success of the reformers and the sympathies of crown and court, Protestantism was still the religion of a minority.

Edward's early death brought Henry's daughter Mary to the throne. A devout Catholic married to the heir to the Spanish throne, her religious policy was as clear-cut as Edward's. The spread of Protestantism was to be halted and Catholicism restored. Catholic bishops were reinstated, Edward's religious legislation was revoked and new heresy laws were enacted, under which nearly three hundred Protestant men and women were executed.

Yet despite Mary's personal convictions, political alliances and forceful policies, ultimately, she failed to achieve her goals. For, as Guy notes of Mary, "A more experienced politician would have paid attention to the anti-papal and anti-Spanish xenophobia that Henry VIII's propaganda had made part of England's culture."[2] That Mary was not only Catholic but married to a Spaniard left her doubly exposed to the power of these ideas. Also, while popular Protestantism was far from universal, where it was strong it ran deep and was held with profound conviction. The identity of the Marian Martyrs, many of them ordinary London wage labourers and many of them relatively young, demonstrates the extent to which Protestantism had taken root among ordinary men and women. Mary's death after only five years on the throne brought the attempt to restore Catholicism to an end.

It was left to Henry's other daughter and Mary's half sister Elizabeth I to define the nature of the English religious settlement, a settlement that emphatically asserted England's Protestantism.

Elizabeth I

While not a zealous Protestant, Elizabeth did favour moderate reform. The cornerstone of this was the Settlement of 1559, which established a national church in England with the monarch as Supreme Governor. Bishops who refused to accept the reforms were replaced - usually by men of strong Protestant conviction. The Prayerbook of 1552 became the required basis of worship, while the 39 Articles of 1563 asserted the theological basis of the national church. Commissions of visitation were sent out into the cities and villages of England to oversee the imposition of the Settlement.

Alongside the official reform movement, the new freedom under Elizabeth gave rise to a populist reform movement. Fuelled by John Foxe's Acts and Monuments - popularly known as Foxe's Book of Martyrs - and the Geneva Bible - an English translation made by Marian exiles - Protestantism continued to widen and deepen its place within English society. By the 1570's England was awash with catechisms and tracts. Ballads extolling the virtues of the English church were sung to popular tunes. These materials "identified the Anglican church with patriotism, depicting Englishmen as God's chosen people."[3]

Despite this, Catholicism remained strong - especially in the early years of Elizabeth's reign. However, the Catholic gentry chose not to constall front the monarchy and professed their loyalty whilst practising occasional conformity. This was the practice of attending the Anglican church sufficiently often to satisfy the authorities while remaining Catholic in their private devotions. The Catholic clergy withdrew into the homes of the gentry and ministered to Catholics from there. Thus Catholicism survived but was increasingly marginalised and constrained. As a result, its ability to sustain itself as a community was dramatically impaired. However, this tolerance had its limits. Those Catholics considered dangerous to the settlement were subjected to the full force of anti-Catholic legislation, especially during times of crisis.

Throughout Elizabeth's reign England was increasingly drawn into wider European conflicts in which matters of religion were just as fundamental as they were in England. In particular, England faced the political and religious threat of Spain.

The Spanish Threat and The Succession

Elizabeth's childlessness made the issue of succession crucial, especially since the strongest claim to the throne was that of a Catholic, Mary Stuart. Fears of a plot to assassinate the Queen and install Mary were far from groundless. Throughout the 1570's and 1580's a succession of plots against Elizabeth were uncovered, some involving agents of the Spanish government. One such plot in 1586 was particularly disturbing for two reasons. First, there was evidence that Mary Stuart herself was involved and, second, it came not long after another major Protestant leader in Europe - William of Orange - had fallen victim to an assassin.

Protestant fears were compounded by the promulgation of the papal bull *Regnans in Excelsis*. This bull excommunicated Elizabeth, relieved English Catholics of their obligation towards her and encouraged them to overthrow her. However, the bull was a disaster. Philip of Spain - the only Catholic monarch powerful enough to attempt to enforce the bull in England - was not minded to do so. English Catholics who had managed to survive, if not flourish, were placed in an impossible position. Worse still, the bull "created an inexorable logic for Elizabeth: that Protestants were loyal and Catholics traitors."[4]

The repeated plots and the papal bull provoked a much harsher policy against Catholicism. Treason laws were enacted and enforced against Jesuits and priests trained in foreign seminaries, with many being executed. Mary Stuart herself was executed in 1587. Mary's execution, in turn, provoked a sharp upturn in hostility with Spain. Plans for an invasion of England had long been in Spanish minds, and the plan was put into effect in 1588. An armada of Spanish ships carrying an invasion force sailed for England. They never made it. The 'Protestant Wind' came to the assistance of the English fleet and the Spanish were scattered.

For the Protestants of England this was nothing short of a miracle. God was safeguarding their Settlement, their church and their freedom. Protestantism was vindicated, and the sense of God's blessing on the nation was reinforced. Subsequently, England joined in much more forcefully on the side of Europe's Protestants, supporting both the Netherlands and the Protestant claimant to the French throne against Philip of Spain and the Catholic League. Elizabeth may have wanted to stay out of these European conflicts, but England was inexorably drawn into the Protestant camp. This involvement, together with the defeat of the Armada, "did much to forge the links between Protestantism and national identity."[5]

Protestantism and Catholicism in Sixteenth Century England

In Tudor England the notion that religion and politics constituted separate spheres was incomprehensible. There was, rather, an intimate and critical connection between religion and public life - religion was politics and politics was religion. Moreover, the political identity of England throughout this period was increasingly interpreted through the nation's religious identity, and that religious identity was Protestant.

THE GLORIOUS REVOLUTION

England under the Stuarts[6]

The sixteenth century almost began with a bang. In 1605 The Gunpowder Plot was thwarted when Guy Fawkes was arrested in a cellar beneath the Houses of Parliament. He and his Catholic co-conspirators were executed for treason while England rejoiced at its providential deliverance.

James I, the target of the plotters, survived but throughout his reign tension was rising between king and parliament. His son Charles succeeded him in 1625, and during his reign tensions rose still further. His cavalier attitude to parliament, his favouring of his French Catholic wife's friends at court and his attempt to impose uniformity in religion on Scotland dragged England into a civil war which ended with his execution.

After the Restoration in 1660 Charles' son - also Charles - ascended the throne. Parliament remained deeply concerned at the direction of Charles II's religious policies and with good cause. For Charles had signed a secret treaty with France promising to reintroduce Catholicism in return for support in his war against the Dutch. Of greater concern was his son James who became king in 1685. A more zealous Catholic he attempted to do what his father had promised but never carried out - return England to Catholicism. Parliament turned against him, and the stage was set for the Glorious Revolution.

The Glorious Revolution

The Protestant wind that blew in 1588 to scatter England's Catholic enemies blew again in 1688 to speed its Protestant deliverer. On November 5 of that year William of Orange landed at Torbay in Devon. Ostensibly, William had come to England at the invitation of some of its leading politicians to investigate the state of the nation's laws and liberties. In reality William's landing was an invasion designed to forestall another Anglo-French alliance against the Dutch.

15

Before he landed Dutch propagandists were in full swing. In a declaration published in October 1688 William explained his actions and intentions. He had been invited to inquire into the condition of civil and religious liberties. He stressed the need to protect established religion, maintain the independence of the judiciary and secure the election of a free parliament. In addition there were dark hints concerning the circumstances of the arrival of James' newborn heir - James Francis Edward Stuart. William called for an investigation in order to protect the succession rights of his wife Mary, James' daughter.

William expected a pitched battle with the forces of James but James fled, eventually escaping to the safety of France. James' flight created chaos. In particular, it created constitutional chaos. Was he king or not? If not, was his new born son king? Had he abdicated? Was the throne vacant? William's English supporters were convinced that if he had not come Protestantism would have withered away in England. But now that he was there they did not know what to do with him. And so parliament set to work "to find a way to fit reality within their principles."[7]

After a period of intense debate Lords and Commons together declared William and Mary king and queen of England. The principles underlying their decision were set out in the Declaration of Rights read at their enthronement. And so England's Protestant parliament and England's Protestant monarch had secured the well being of the Protestant kingdom.

What had James done? Why did conservative Anglicans, believing in the hereditary principle and only too aware of the traumas of the constitutional crisis less than fifty years earlier, set aside the hereditary principle and risk renewed crisis? The Declaration of Rights asserted that "it hath been found by experience that it is inconsistent with the safety and welfare of the Protestant kingdom to be governed by a popish prince." The experience referred to was primarily the experience of the preceding three years under James II.

James was a convinced Catholic. However, his accession was accepted on the basis that he would rule by established law and maintain the independence of the Anglican church. In addition, James' heir at that time was his Protestant daughter Mary, husband of William of Orange.

James, however, lacked his father's political judgement and pushed to the limit his plans to allow for the open practice of Catholicism. In pursuit of his goal James did not shrink from using his powers of patronage to advance his allies and impede his opponents. When parliament would not accede to his wishes he used his own authority to appoint Catholics to the court, to the magistracy, to the militia and to the universities. The church was brought under the control of a Commission for Ecclesiastical Causes, and James attempted to circumvent the refusal of the church to countenance his pro-Catholic policy by creating an alliance with Dissenters - non-Anglican Protestants. But most dissenters were wary, having little doubt that James was merely using them for his own ends.

Consequently, when William landed on England's shores neither Anglicans nor Dissenters would rally to the support of their king. James' rule and William's accession "revealed the bedrock of commitment to the Protestant religion and the fault-lines along which belief in an indefeasible hereditary succession would crack."[8] When it came to a choice of upholding the hereditary principle - a principle at the core of the English constitution - or upholding Protestantism, even the most conservative elements in English society chose Protestantism.[9]

Protestantism and Catholicism in Seventeenth Century England

"Popery," writes Kishlansky in his history of seventeenth century Britain, "was a familiar trope of English political life."[10] Though the Catholic population of England continued to decline throughout the century popery remained the enemy within. Popery had burned the English martyrs, had sent an armada against England and had incited the Gunpowder Plot, the Irish rebellion and the Great Fire of London.

On the fifth of November all England celebrated deliverance from Rome, burning effigies of the Catholic conspirator Guy Fawkes. On 17th November, England celebrated Queen Elizabeth's Day with more bonfires and effigies, this time of the Pope. England's greatness was forged against the constant subversions of Rome.

And Popery was the enemy without. England faced the Catholic powers of France and Spain ready to do the bidding of Rome. More than this, Rome threatened not only through direct invasion by Catholic states but through stealth, conspiracy and infiltration. In pursuit of its goals Rome's agents were held to have committed all manner of cruelties. England, then, was a state under siege, constantly aware of the power and presence and danger of Rome. "Popery was everyone's nightmare; thus anti-popery was omnipresent."[11]

More and more, Englishness came to be seen in terms of Protestantism. Catholicism was increasingly viewed as something alien and dangerous. English Protestants came to see their survival and the failure of Catholic conspiracies as signs of God's providential care for the nation. This was a generation that looked on England's Catholic past as another time and another place.

AN UNCOMPROMISING PROTESTANTISM[12]

Jacobite Risings and Wars with France

Britain entered the eighteenth century as a state whose constitution, monarch, parliament and church asserted their Protestantism. The construction of this Protestant state began in 1688 but was not completed until 1714. In 1701 the Act of Settlement barred Catholics and those married to Catholics from ascending to the throne. In 1707 Scotland and England were united through the Act of Union. In 1714, following the death of Mary's sister and James' daughter Anne, parliament passed over a host of claimants to the British throne and chose as their King, George, the Elector of Hanover. George could speak little English and had never visited the country. Throughout his reign he was more concerned with the politics of his European possessions than those of his new kingdom. However, George was Protestant. And while he was Protestant in the Lutheran way, it was his Protestantism rather than his Lutheranism that mattered most.

In reality Britain had become a constitutional monarchy, if not an elective monarchy - though the constitutional documents and the political theorists tended to play this down. And at the heart of the constitution lay the assertion of the Protestant character of the nation. As Colley notes, "Not only was succession to the throne conditional on the monarch belonging to the Protestant faith, but the people's allegiance was conditional on his abiding by the constitution."[13]

Yet despite the apparently decisive nature of 1688, Britain was still an insecure nation. The descendants of James II were alive and well in France. They still harboured a desire to reclaim the throne. The Catholic Stuarts supported by Catholic France threatened the stability of the Protestant state. Three times in the eighteenth century the Stuarts attempted to regain the throne by force.

The first two attempts in 1708 and 1715 made little impact, but a more serious rising took place in 1745. Charles Edward Stuart landed in Scotland and Jacobite forces advanced to within 120 miles of London. At that point they chose to withdraw and at Culloden the Jacobites were defeated and then routed. Charles Edward sailed off to France and into myth.

However, what really concerned Britain was not the Jacobites - despite their initial successes - but the French. Britain was at war with France for a total of sixty-nine years in the period between 1689 and 1815. The longest period of peace lasted for thirty years. Even then, the struggle between Britain and France continued by other means. Until at least 1748 religion was a key element in these wars since one of France's objectives was the restoration of the Stuarts. Consequently, on the British side, "all of these wars were bound to raise the issue of the security of the Protestant settlement within Great Britain itself."[14] France had replaced Spain as the 'other' against which the British nation defined itself. France, like Spain before it, represented the forces of Catholicism alien to and at enmity with Britain's Protestantism.

Rule Britannia

God preserved Protestant England from the Jacobites and the French. Survival then turned to triumph in the Seven Years War (1756-63). The defeat of the French in North America, India and elsewhere "represented a high-point of imperial achievement."[15]

Britain's survival and expansion was reflected and celebrated in popular song - songs still sung today. In 1740 James Thomson, the son of a Scottish minister wrote,

When Britain first at Heaven's command,
Arose from out the azure main;
This was the charter of the land,
And guardian angels sang this strain;
Rule, Britannia! Britannia, rule the waves:
Britons never will be slaves.

Here Britain's divine origins and providential survival were named and celebrated. If Britain was now a world power, if the horrors of a Catholic king had been avoided, if the terrifying other - France - had been held and defeated, it was because God was Britain's God and the British were his people. Yes, England, Scotland and Wales differed in the nature of their religious settlements, but over and above any difference when confronted with the Catholic other they were one in their Protestantism.

This shared religious allegiance unified the people of Britain and at the same time distinguished them from the French. It was this shared allegiance combined with recurring wars against the French "that permitted a sense of British national identity to emerge," writes Colley. "Protestantism," she continues, "was the dominant component of British religious life. Protestantism coloured the way that Britons approached and interpreted their material life. Protestantism determined how most Britons viewed their politics. And an uncompromising Protestantism was the foundation on which their state was explicitly and unapologetically based."[16]

Cycles of Time

Moreover, the strength of this ideology lay not only in its ability to explain the present, but to integrate the present with the past. The British people lived by a calendar of celebrations that constantly confronted them with two inescapable realities - the providential blessing of being Protestant and the constant threat from Catholicism. "Time past was a soap opera written by God, a succession of warning disasters and providential escapes which they acted out afresh every year as a way of reminding themselves who they were."[17]

Events in the wider world also contributed to the assertion of the connection of Protestantism with Britishness. It was, after all, only since the Glorious Revolution that Britain had risen to the status of a world power and finally achieved a decisive victory over Catholic Europe. What else could this be but the blessing of God? Britons, hearing of famine, ignorance and the subjugation of the population in Catholic lands believed themselves to be freer, richer and better off as a consequence of Protestantism - and to a degree this was true.

Events overseas also helped to confirm the Protestant view of Catholicism. French Huguenots, expelled from France in 1685, had arrived on British shores with tales of terror at the hands of church and state in France. In the eighteenth century the Inquisition was about its work in Spain. In some of the German states and in parts of the Austrian Empire Protestants were under pressure. All of this was reported in the British press and circulated in pamphlets. Catholicism was not, in the eyes of the British people or their rulers, simply another religion, but an aggressive political power advocating an ideology fundamentally at odds with that of the British, Protestant state.

Anti-Catholicism

Anti-catholicism was still a dominant aspect of British life in the first part of the eighteenth century, especially in light of the perceived threat from the Jacobites and the French. Yet as the century wore on, events began to reshape perceptions of Catholicism among both government and social elites.

First, Britain's successes against France in the Seven Years War left the nation as a global power. This war also finally put an end to all hopes for the return of the Stuart dynasty. Second, Britain's victory in North America brought a huge population of French speaking Catholics under British authority. Somehow this community had to be accommodated. Third, the revolution in France transformed Britain's historic enemy from a conservative Catholic state to a revolutionary and radical state. Britain and France would fight more wars, but France was no longer the Catholic 'other'.

As a consequence the situation of Catholics in Britain improved both formally with the passing of a measure of relief in 1778, and informally. However, while elites may have been changing their perceptions the extent of anti-catholicism among the wider population was still significant. The Act of 1778 led directly to the Gordon Riots – "the most destructive and intolerantly Protestant of all British riots."[18] In all 285 people were killed, 173 wounded, 450 arrested and 35 executed. Britain was still Protestant and that Protestantism was still capable of considerable militancy when the circumstances arose. And on the horizon was another movement which would give a fresh impetus to British Protestantism - evangelicalism.

ENGLAND IN THE NINETEENTH CENTURY[19]

The nineteenth century is marked by both continuity and discontinuity in the relationship between Protestantism and British identity. A number of key factors helped define the nature of the relationship. First, there was the consolidation of the Empire. The global expansion of the eighteenth century continued in the nineteenth century,

Britain was clearly the world's superpower, dominant both economically and militarily. Second, there was the rise of evangelicalism. This movement gave a new edge to Britain's Protestantism, both in its affirmation of the centrality of Protestantism for British identity and in its hostility towards Catholicism. Third, there was the increasingly problematic relationship with Ireland occasioned by the rise of Irish nationalism - both as a mass movement in Ireland and as a parliamentary movement in Westminster - and by the huge influx of Irish Catholics into British cities.

Empire[20]

"The idea that Britain had received the Empire as a providential gift of God for the diffusion of Christianity and civilization had a long pedigree in nineteenth century thought."[21] Empire was both a gift and a responsibility. So *The Churchman*, an evangelical Anglican periodical, argued in its golden jubilee edition of 1887 that Britain had been chosen and providentially made fit by God "for spreading His glory among the nations."[22]

There was no need to spell out the nature of the Christianity that Britain was duty bound to spread. It was that same Protestant Christianity that had made Britain great and that was the greatest force for civilization and liberty. Mission societies sprung up across Britain to go to the farthest corners of the great Empire with the message of the gospel. Missionaries like David Livingstone joined the pantheon of Protestant heroes.

But the Empire itself pointed to another more fundamental reality. It witnessed to a nation that was entering into its full glory. Economically and militarily Britain reigned supreme at home and abroad. Britain stood alone through much of the nineteenth century as the world's leading and only superpower.

One consequence of this was that the nation's relationship with Catholicism changed. In the first place Catholics had played their part in building and running this Empire. But more than that, Britain could

23

no longer see itself as a threatened and vulnerable nation surrounded by the hostile forces of Catholicism. Catholicism was neither an internal nor an external threat. Consequently, in 1829 the British parliament passed the Emancipation Act giving both civil and political liberties to Britain's Catholics.

However, it would be wrong to assume that the passing of this Act severed the relationship between British identity and Protestantism. While the Act of 1829 did not provoke the violence that the much more limited Act of 1778 had done, it was still opposed by a great many in parliament and among the ordinary people.

In particular, parliament was flooded with local petitions opposing emancipation. Some of these came from cities like Glasgow and Liverpool where increasing Irish immigration exacerbated existing religious conflict by provoking both ethnic conflict and economic grievance. But many others came from the town and villages of England where Catholics were rare and Irish Catholics non-existent. For these ordinary Britons "Protestantism was a vital part of who they were…and the frame through which they looked at the past."[23]

The British State, too, displayed a similar kind of reaction in 1850 in response to Pius IX's recreation of the Catholic episcopacy in Britain. Opposition and outrage followed Pius' announcement - not only on the streets but in Protestant churches and in parliament. Ordinary citizens gathered at public meetings to sign petitions, with November 5th providing a particular focus. In the churches clergy preached against Rome and Catholicism drawing on the annals of Protestant Britain's conflict with Catholicism through the centuries.

In parliament these events - which came to be known as The Papal Aggression - were repeatedly debated and roundly denounced. The Prime Minister, Lord John Russell, expressed his views forcefully in a letter to the Bishop of Durham which was subsequently published in *The Times*. "The liberty of Protestantism," wrote the Prime Minister, "has been enjoyed too long in England to allow of any successful attempt to impose a foreign yoke upon our minds and consciences."[24]

The British state may have redefined its relationship with its Catholic citizens in 1829 but, in the minds of both rulers and people, the link between Protestantism and British identity remained strong.

Evangelicalism[25]

Evangelicalism gave a new energy to British Protestantism. However, evangelicalism also stood in continuity with British Protestantism. Evangelicals, too, held the common conviction that Britain was a great nation because it was a Protestant nation. Evangelicals, too, held the common Protestant perception of Catholicism as impoverishing and illiberal. Indeed, evangelicalism's intense concern for theology heightened the movement's opposition to Catholicism. Biblical authority was proclaimed over against the authority of the Catholic church. The necessity of conversion was stressed and the sacramentalism of Catholicism condemned. The missionary zeal of many evangelicals led them to see the Empire as God's gift for the evangelisation of the nations.

However, despite these continuities, evangelical responses to Catholic emancipation were mixed. Some were totally opposed to any measure of emancipation, some were ambivalent, while others actively supported emancipation. Since many evangelicals were non-conformists and had themselves been subject to discriminatory legislation, they saw emancipation as a matter of civil justice. They also recognised the difficulty of proclaiming their own liberality while discriminating against their Catholic fellow citizens.

Yet, whatever their view of emancipation, the passing of the Act did not significantly alter their view of Catholicism or their understanding of the relationship between Protestantism and British identity. Indeed, now that the Protestant nature of the state was no longer to be enforced through legislation, many evangelicals believed that it could only be maintained through their own activism. Thus 1827 saw the establishment of the Reformation Society, while in 1835 the Protestant Association was established. Both bodies campaigned for Protestantism and against Catholicism, with the former focusing more on the theological issues in dispute and the latter concentrating on the social and political issues.

This evangelical Protestant community was active throughout the middle of the nineteenth century. Evangelicals agitated on behalf of the Church of Ireland against Government reforms which weakened its place in Ireland. They agitated again when the Government increased its financial support to the Catholic seminary at Maynooth. And during the Papal Aggression evangelicals were active once more.

Nor were they mere populists - evangelicals were well represented among the clergy of the Anglican church and many sat in parliament, both in the Commons and the Lords. These evangelical movements worked closely with others, particularly in the Tory Party, on these issues. One consequence of this activism was that religious matters - especially in relation to Ireland – remained central to British politics and significantly impinged on the general election of 1835.

While evangelicalism did not create a mass movement around these issues, it did not have to, since it was able to tap into the general sense of Protestant Britishness which was the norm in nineteenth century society. Evangelicals, in asserting the fundamental role of Protestantism and the fundamental threat from Catholicism, could rely on getting a sympathetic hearing at all levels of British society.

Ireland

Nineteenth-century British politics was conducted against the backdrop of the rising tide of Irish nationalism. While it was the not the sole topic of British politics, it was a crucial one, especially in the latter part of the century. The rise of Parnell's Irish Party in the British parliament and the personal commitment of William Ewart Gladstone – the dominant political figure of the late nineteenth century – to the resolution of Ireland's dispute with England ensured that British politics would remain focused on Ireland as a core, rather than a merely peripheral, issue.

Irish agitation had earlier found a voice in the campaigns of Daniel O'Connell for Catholic emancipation and repeal of the Act of Union. A well-organised pattern of protest came to a peak with the election of O'Connell to the British parliament at a by-election in 1828. As a Catholic he was prohibited from taking his seat. And so the matter of emancipation moved centre stage. O'Connell consolidated the position of Irish issues in the British parliament in the election of 1832 when thirty-nine of his supporters were returned from Ireland.

O'Connell's commitment to repeal did not waver, but in the meantime he turned his thoughts to other more achievable goals. One of these goals was to reduce the power and influence of the Church of Ireland and O'Connell harnessed the vigour of an existing protest movement to that end. As a result, in 1833, parliament passed the Irish Church Temporalities Act. This Act, with its implications for the principle of establishment, became a core issue in political debate at the time of the 1835 British general election.

Despite some successes O'Connell's movement for repeal came to nothing. Then, in the late 1850's and 1860's the pursuit of Irish aspirations took a more sinister turn with the rise of the Fenian movement. The Fenians were a secret movement dedicated to the overthrow of British rule in Ireland. Abortive risings in North America and Ireland in 1867 demonstrated the weakness of the movement, but their ability to detonate bombs in England shocked the British public. Worse still, a Fenian attempt to rescue a captured compatriot in Manchester resulted in the death of a police officer. Three of those responsible were executed and their deaths generated a huge wave of public sympathy in Ireland. "The Fenian movement in no sense represented Irish opinion generally, but the danger that it might come to do so encouraged Liberal politicians, especially Gladstone, to concessionary action."[26]

A series of reforms followed: disestablishment of the Church of Ireland, the Land Act of 1870 and the attempted reform of the educational system in 1873. But the Irish campaign had moved on. In 1870

Isaac Butt formed the Home Government Association and changed the shape of Irish and British politics for the next fifty years. In the election of 1874, fifty-nine Home Rulers were returned as opposed to only ten liberals. In 1880 Charles Stewart Parnell became leader of the Home Rule movement and forged a political alliance with Gladstone and the Liberals to deliver Home Rule for Ireland. The general election of 1885 brought the Liberals to power with the support of the Home Rulers and saw the first Home Rule Bill (1886) brought before parliament. Its failure led to the resignation of the government and a new election.

The election was fought on the Home Rule issue. Once again Ireland endorsed Parnell and the Home Rule movement but Britain rejected it. Gladstone and the Liberals returned to opposition and Salisbury came to power as leader of a Conservative government. Home Rule was off the political agenda for the next eight years until Gladstone returned to power once more in 1892.

Throughout the nineteenth century, then, Ireland's relationship with England was a defining political issue. This issue defined political debate and dominated general elections. And, as we have seen, often these issues had distinctly religious dimensions: emancipation, disestablishment, the Maynooth grant.

England's Protestant identity may have undergone radical change in the nineteenth century. However, that identity was still socially and politically significant and it was still central to the awkward relationship of Britain and Ireland.

CONCLUSION

It is impossible to fully understand English and British history since the reformation without significant reference to the role of religion in general and Protestantism in particular. While in its early years English Protestantism was far from universally accepted or strong in its own right, Protestantism gradually came to form a central core of British identity. Naturally that identity changed and developed over the period of four centuries, and the nature of Protestantism and the relationship between the two changed with it. What did not change, however, was the centrality of Protestantism for British citizens, British society and British politics.

In particular Britain's Protestant history and Protestant identity impinged on Britain's relationship with Ireland, especially when a section of that British Protestant community was established in Ireland itself. It is these British Protestants of North East Ireland and their response to the evolving British-Irish relationship in the late nineteenth and early twentieth centuries that are the focus of the next chapter.

2

A FEARFUL PEOPLE

Protestant Ireland in the

Nineteenth Century

CATHOLIC REVIVAL

The significance of the Catholic church for the politics of nineteenth-century Ireland is clearly demonstrated by its role in Daniel O'Connell's campaigns for Catholic emancipation and for the repeal of the Union. The Catholic Association, formed in 1823, was a crucial vehicle of the emancipation movement. The battle for emancipation was fought on two fronts - electoral politics and mass agitation. On both, O'Connell's movement created new alliances between the community and the Catholic clergy. While many liberal or non-conformist Protestants had themselves been advocates of emancipation, O'Connell's creation of an alliance between church and people resulted in a movement that was almost exclusively Catholic.

Following the success of the emancipation campaign, O'Connell turned his attention to a variety of matters which were held to be unjust. One of these concerned the status of the established church. All Irish taxpayers had to contribute to the upkeep of the Church of Ireland. Agrarian protest movements, supported by O'Connell, resisted these demands. The result was the Irish Church Temporalities Act (1833) which, while not changing the Church of Ireland's established status, did significantly reduce the hierarchy - and therefore the costs - of the church. Inevitably, many Protestants saw this as a Catholic campaign against Protestantism in Ireland.

The model that had successfully achieved emancipation was used again in the campaign for repeal of the Act of Union. Electoral politics were combined with popular protest and a broad alliance was created which included the Catholic church and its clergy. The British Government's response was to try to separate clergy from political protest through granting concessions. The most controversial of these was the decision in 1845 to increase significantly the grant to Maynooth College. The British Government considered that clergy trained at Maynooth would be more pliable and loyal since they would be less exposed to the radical ideas they might encounter if they studied in Europe.

O'Connell, then, created a broad alliance that included the church in pursuit of his political goals. However, the result was that the movements O'Connell created and encouraged were overwhelmingly Catholic. "O'Connell," argues Alvin Jackson, "politicized the Irish people using the most accessible tools: the Catholic faith and the Catholic clergy."[1]

The rise of the Home Rule movement under Isaac Butt and Charles Stewart Parnell was initially met by the Catholic hierarchy with a mixture of suspicion and hostility, on the grounds that it was a plot to discredit and undermine the Catholic church. However, this hostility did not last. Parnell knew that he needed the support of the church and worked hard to establish a relationship with the hierarchy. The death of Cardinal Paul Cullen, who remained suspicious of the Home Rule movement, created new possibilities for that relationship.

Subsequently, the Catholic clergy and hierarchy became more closely involved with the Home Rule movement and this growing commitment culminated in the church's endorsement of Home Rule in 1886. However, the price that Parnell paid for the support of the church was the expunging from his campaign of anything the church might find objectionable, especially in the area of education. The result was a movement that gained the support of the Catholic church but alienated the Protestants of Ireland.

If Irish nationalism was increasingly well-organised and self-confident through the nineteenth century, so too was Irish Catholicism. While this transformation was underway in the early part of the century, its greatest impact was seen in the latter part when, in the aftermath of the famine, Paul Cullen was consecrated as Archbishop of Armagh.

Cullen, though born in Ireland, studied in Rome and was then appointed as a lecturer. For eighteen years he served as Rector of Rome's Irish College. During his time in Rome he became a friend of Giovanni Maria Mastai-Ferretti, who would become Pope in 1846. As Pope

Pius IX he opposed political and religious liberalism, asserted and strengthened the authority of the papacy over the Catholic church world wide and convened the First Vatican Council which promulgated the dogma of Papal Infallibility. The nineteenth century Catholic revival, driven by Pius, "reinforced…[Catholicism's] medieval and anti-Protestant characteristics."[2]

Cullen was consecrated as Archbishop of Armagh in 1850 and then Archbishop of Dublin in 1852, finally being made the first Cardinal of Ireland in 1867. Until his death in 1878 Cullen worked for the implementation of the vision of Pius IX in Ireland. One of his first acts was to convene the Synod of Thurles in 1850. At the Synod "the bishops agreed to strengthen their collective authority and the supremacy of the Pope; to regularise devotional practice and root out religious customs of doubtful Christian origin; to launch a counter-attack on second Reformation missionary activity; to insist that Protestant partners marrying Catholics guarantee that all their children be brought up as Catholics; and to campaign for denominational education at every level."[3]

Cullen's personal links did most to strengthen the Irish church's ties with Rome, while Catholic missionary orders brought errant Catholics back into the fold. Missions became a regular feature of Catholic life and parochial societies maintained zeal and faithfulness among the laity. Roman devotional practices were introduced and became the norm. Mass attendance became almost universal and new Catholic churches were built to cope with the upsurge in religious observation.

At a political level, too, Cullen was active. While still Rector of the Irish College, Cullen supported those in the Irish hierarchy who rejected the Academical Institutions (Ireland) Bill (1845) which established a number of non-denominational Queen's Colleges in Ireland to provide higher level education. Instead, Cullen campaigned for the creation of a Catholic University of Ireland. Cullen also campaigned for the creation of a comprehensive system of state funded denominational education.

As for the national question, Cullen subsumed all political matters to the interests of his vision of Irish Catholicism. Thus Cullen opposed Fenianism seeing it as liberal, radical and anti-clerical. He tried to create an alternative political movement - the National Association of Ireland - to campaign on Disestablishment, state funding of Catholic education and tenants' rights. However, it failed to make a political impact. The church that Cullen left at his death in 1878 was strong, well-organised, popular, authoritarian and illiberal. It was all that Protestants imagined and feared the Catholic church to be. Consequently, when the church allied itself to the Home Rule movement some year later the Protestant reaction was inevitable. Home Rule would very certainly be Rome Rule.

PROTESTANT REACTION

Irish Protestantism in the nineteenth century faced a very different situation from that facing Protestants in the rest of the United Kingdom. In England Roman Catholics were few in number and politically irrelevant. Britain's traditional enemies presented no serious threat to the nation, Britain itself being the dominant military and political power. Consequently Catholicism was no longer perceived as a threat either internally or externally.

This did not mean that Britain was no longer self-consciously a Protestant nation, nor that anti-Catholicism was no longer common in all levels of society, nor that the British view of Catholicism had changed. It meant simply that Britain's relationship with Catholicism was interpreted from a position of strength and confidence rather than fear and weakness. As a result the fear of Catholicism was no longer the defining element in British politics.

However, Irish Protestants faced a very different situation. Roman Catholics constituted the overwhelming majority of the population. And, if at the beginning of the nineteenth century their political power was limited and the church enfeebled, the story of the nineteenth century is the story of the attempt to gain for Irish Catholics political power commensurate with their numerical strength. Moreover, this political transformation was set against the background of an increasingly well organised and increasingly socially and theologically conservative Catholic church.

Nineteenth century Irish Protestantism was therefore pulled in two directions. On the one hand Irish Protestants identified with the Kingdom and the Empire. They saw themselves as an integral part of a great and glorious Protestant Kingdom and Empire with all the responsibilities and privileges that came with that. Thus Irish Protestants had reason for confidence and pride when they looked outward.

Looking inwards, however, told a different story. They saw themselves confronted by a political movement that seemed to threaten the basis of all that they held dear - the Union with Britain. Irish Protestants feared for the survival of the Union and the survival of its values of liberty and progress in an island separated from Britain and dominated by a politically active and theologically conservative, authoritarian and anti-Protestant Roman Catholic church. Looking inward, Irish Protestantism's pride and confidence very rapidly gave way to fear and suspicion.

This in turn had two implications for the Irish Protestants' relationship with Britain. First, it became increasingly difficult to persuade the British people and parliament of the seriousness of the situation facing Irish Protestants. As the British and Irish experiences of Catholicism began to diverge, so did the response to Catholicism. In particular, the pattern of political development diverged significantly. Irish political life, which had been developing along British party lines, was shattered and evolved into the sectarian politics that is still with us.

Second, British and Irish anti-Catholicism went separate ways. Anti-Catholicism was still a central part of British self-understanding and of the Constitution, but, in the absence of any real Catholic threat, its role in political life declined. In Ireland, however, anti-Catholicism remained a potent political force given the threat from Catholicism, both as a movement of political activism and as a religiously conservative and authoritarian body.

Henry Cooke and Protestant Union[4]

Irish Protestantism in the nineteenth century reacted strongly to what it perceived as the renewed threat from Catholicism. At the heart of that reaction in the first half of the century was the Presbyterian minister Henry Cooke.

Cooke first came to prominence in the 1820's through his dogged opposition to ministers within his own denomination whose views of Christ he considered heretical. Eventually, in 1829, the disputes over this issue split Presbyterianism, with those whom Cooke was opposing choosing to leave before they were expelled. This split left Irish Presbyterianism a theologically and politically more coherent - if narrower - body. Cooke was to remain a central figure within Presbyterianism until his death in 1868.

Cooke's concerns were not limited solely to questions of the doctrinal orthodoxy of Presbyterianism. Cooke was also concerned by the growing political and religious power of Catholicism. Cooke and his supporters believed Catholicism to be a false religion, a repressive social phenomenon, and a threat, not only to Ireland, but to Britain and the Empire as well.

More than this, Cooke had reason to believe that Catholicism was on the rise once more and that the government lacked both an understanding of the risks from resurgent Catholicism and the political will to resist it. The Emancipation and Reform Acts and the threat to the establishment of the Church of Ireland convinced him that Protestants in Ireland had to set aside their theological and denominational differences and unite in support of the established church and against the threat from Catholicism.

Cooke expressed his concerns and called for unity most notably at a rally held in 1834 to protest against encroachments on the privileges of the Church of Ireland. At a time when mutual dislike between Presbyterians and the Church of Ireland was common and when Presbyterians were generally hostile to the establishment principle, Cooke's position was a radical one. Cooke was to pursue this goal for the rest of his life. Even as an old and frail man he attended and addressed a rally in 1867 in support of the establishment of the Church of Ireland.

While many within Presbyterianism had little sympathy with the established church and less desire for a Protestant Union this was not because they were any the less concerned about the danger of Catholicism. More often it was because they believed that the Church of Ireland could not be the bulwark against Catholicism that was necessary. However, despite these fears and the old resentments Cooke did live to see his Protestant vision take shape - at least in an informal way - through the impact of evangelicalism.

Evangelicalism was making inroads in both the Presbyterian Church in Ireland and the Church of Ireland. Despite differences over doctrine, church order and relations with the state, and despite previous hostility between the two communions, clergy and congregations from both these and other Protestant denominations increasingly shared a common evangelicalism. Moreover, members of these different denominations found themselves working side by side in the host of interdenominational agencies that had sprung up in the early nineteenth century. Common religious experience and common religious aspirations were breaking down the barriers and there was little those who opposed such change could do to prevent it. Evangelicalism was proving to be a more dynamic force than denominational and confessional allegiance.

More than this, evangelicalism brought with it a common anti-Catholicism. This evangelical anti-catholicism tapped into the national anti-catholicism of British Protestantism. Evangelicals, too, believed that Britain was providentially kept and blessed by God for its adherence to Protestant truth and had a responsibility to act accordingly. Evangelicals, too, believed that Catholicism was socially, politically and theologically reactionary and repressive. But evangelicals brought to anti-catholicism a heightened sense of the theological distinction between Catholicism and Protestantism.

Evangelicalism thus had a dual effect. On the one hand it broke down the barriers between Protestants. On the other hand evangelicalism sustained and reinforced the sense of difference from Catholicism. This dual phenomenon was to be seen even more clearly as a consequence of Irish evangelicalism's greatest moment - the 1859 revival.

The 1859 Revival[5]

"Before it happened it was longingly anticipated, after it happened it was nostalgically remembered, and ever after it became a litmus test of the spiritual vigour of evangelical religion."[6]

The revival in Ireland was part of a series of transatlantic revivals which began in 1858 in the USA. In that year the General Assembly of the Presbyterian Church focused on the hope of revival and issued a call to prayer and preparation for revival. The church also despatched two ministers to the US to observe events there.

In March 1859 what began as a slow and fairly low-key movement primarily within Presbyterianism broke out into a revival. The centre of the movement was in County Antrim. Churches were packed. Men and women were physically overcome as they confessed sin and prayed for forgiveness. Beyond the church buildings and the regular services informal prayer and testimony meetings multiplied in peoples' homes and in the open air. Not just the clergy, but ordinary churchgoers - including some only recently converted - preached to their friends and neighbours.

The revival movement spread first to other rural areas of Ulster - particularly those where Presbyterianism was strong - and then into the cities and towns. This urban movement was more clearly interdenominational. "Evangelical ministers of different Protestant denominations co-operated in organising open air revival meetings and regular union prayer meetings, which served to weaken barriers and blur theological distinctions."[7] Urban revivalism also produced a series of mass rallies, the biggest being held in Belfast's Botanic Gardens in June when an estimated 35,000 people attended.

The events in Ulster attracted international attention. Well known evangelists from Britain and the US came to speak. Clergy from Scotland and England came to help manage the masses who had converted. And lay people came from around the world to observe and experience the events.

As well as filling the churches, the revival had other consequences - at least in the short term. There was an emphasis on moral reform which reflected the traditional concerns of Protestant communities. There was an emphasis on Sabbath observance. Public houses closed. Gambling and other undesirable activities were reduced. There was an emphasis on fulfilling one's duties to others.

Among some, there was a hope that the revival might help overcome the sectarianism of Ulster society which had flared up in 1857 with serious rioting in Belfast. And, indeed, the events of the twelfth of July of that year seem to have been more subdued than normal with some Orangemen opting to attend prayer meetings rather than to parade.

However, the revival's impact on the Catholic population was limited. Few converts came from that community and those that did were generally on the margins to begin with. Moreover, there seems to have been little real commitment on the part of many involved in the revival to try to win Catholics. "Protestants soon ceased to look for extensive Catholic conversions," writes Brown, "especially as Catholics in many districts closed ranks against the revival. There was never much effort invested in proselytising; the revival from the beginning was primarily concerned with the life and faith of Protestant communities."[8]

By the Autumn of 1859 revival activity was slowing down and there was opportunity to take stock of what had happened. Certainly there was a dramatic increase in the number of churchgoers across all the Protestant denominations. However, it was the longer-term changes that the revival brought about that are more significant, for the revival changed the nature of Irish Protestantism. The revival also reshaped the Protestant community by breaking down some barriers and reinforcing others.

The religion of the revival was pietistic, conversionist and individualistic. This represented a significant change from the more communally-based religion of the main Protestant traditions. This individualistic emphasis was common within the wider world of evangelicalism and, indeed, remains a marked feature of much contemporary evangelicalism.

As a result the revival broke down some of the denominational and confessional barriers between Protestants in Ulster. While they were separated by different confessions and different histories, increasingly they were united by a common evangelical experience. And not only did this break down denominational barriers, it also enabled Ulster Protestants to see themselves as part of a much wider evangelical culture that encompassed Britain and the United States. Ulster Protestants were part of a great transatlantic community of faith.

However, if some barriers were being broken down, others were being reinforced. First, the barrier between Ulster and the rest of Ireland was being reinforced. Demography and economic development had already set Ulster apart. Now the revival, confined as it was almost exclusively to Ulster, reinforced those differences. There had been some revival activity among Protestant communities in the rest of Ireland but nothing on the scale of what was seen in Ulster.

At the same time the revival also reinforced barriers within Ulster - the barrier between Protestant and Catholic. God had, after all, passed over the Catholic community in that 'year of grace'. Any reflection on that fact tended to emphasise its implications for the nature of the Catholic community rather than the Protestant community.

Protestantism, then, revived and united, found itself sharing the land with a Catholicism which itself was experiencing the renewal of its life and institutions. Consequently, the revival failed to deliver the expectations of some that sectarianism would be overcome. Only five years later, in 1864, rioting far more severe than that of 1857 wracked Belfast.

Opposition to Home Rule[9]

Growing Protestant concerns over the direction of British government policy came to a head in the 1880's as the Prime Minister, William Ewart Gladstone, introduced the first Home Rule Bill. The Bill, published in 1886, provoked an overwhelmingly hostile reaction from all sections of Irish Protestantism - not least the churches. The Church of Ireland called a special synod and the Presbyterians a special meeting of the General Assembly to debate the Bill. Both bodies produced a series of resolutions strongly critical of the Government's proposals.

The Methodists, too, registered their protest. Their denominational paper, the *Christian Advocate*, proclaimed that "Home Rule for Ireland means not only war against the crown rights of England, but against the crown rights of Christ...its inspiration is religious antipathy, its methods plunder, its object Protestant annihilation."[10]

Nor was it only the mainstream denominations that objected. Congregationalists and Baptists travelled to England with their non-conformist colleagues from Presbyterian and Methodist churches to persuade their fellow non-conformists of the iniquity of Home Rule. And of the 990 non-conformist ministers in Ireland, 864 put their names to an address against Home Rule.

As well as denominational meetings, Ulster Protestants began to organise mass rallies in opposition to Home Rule which cut across divisions of denomination, politics and class among Ulster unionists. The most notable took place in 1892 when 12,000 delegates met in Belfast for a great Convention. The meeting began with prayer from the Anglican Archbishop of Armagh, a Scripture reading from a former Presbyterian moderator and the singing of a Psalm. Two resolutions were proposed - one opposing Home Rule and one expressing sympathy and support for unionists in the other three provinces. Among those proposing or speaking in support of the motions were leading clergy from all the main Protestant denominations in Ireland.

However, what was significant about the demonstration of 1892 is that it brought together the diverse strands of Ulster unionism in opposition to Home Rule. Liberals and conservatives in both politics and religion stood side by side. The Orange Order was present, but only as one strand among the unionist community. The organisers of the Convention, aware of the danger that their opposition could be misrepresented as nothing more than sectarian prejudice, were conscious of the need to demonstrate the breadth and coherence of the unionist opposition to Home Rule.

The renewal of the threat of Home Rule in 1912 provoked another series of rallies and public meetings. On Easter Tuesday of 1912 100,000 gathered in Belfast to hear Bonar Law, leader of the Conservative Party, pledge his support to the unionist cause. Again, at this ostensibly political event the meeting began with prayer, scripture readings and hymn singing, with the Anglican Primate and Presbyterian Moderator leading.

1912 also witnessed a more overtly religious demonstration against Home Rule. This was the Presbyterian Convention held in Belfast in February. An estimated 50,000 Presbyterian men attended this meeting - half the male Presbyterian population of Ulster. The arguments used were by now familiar though there was a distinctive appeal to their fellow Presbyterians in Scotland and a declaration entrusting their cause to God.

Ulster Covenant

Ulster unionism delivered its definitive response to Home Rule on Saturday September 28 1912 - Ulster Day. This was the day set aside for the signing of Ulster's Solemn League and Covenant. The day began in church. Across Ulster Protestant men and women attended services in their local churches before mustering at the appointed places to sign the Covenant. In Belfast, the leaders of Irish unionism held their service in the Ulster Hall before moving to the City Hall for the signing.

At the Ulster Hall the assembled congregation was addressed by Dr William McKean, a former Moderator of the Irish Presbyterian Church. He told them, "The Irish Question is at bottom a war against Protestantism; it is an attempt to establish a Roman Catholic ascendancy in Ireland to begin the disintegration of the Empire by securing a second parliament in Dublin."[11] In this one sentence, Dr McKean drew together the key elements of the Protestant objection to Home Rule.

At the City Hall, Carson was the first to put his name to the Covenant followed by Lord Londonderry. Following the political leaders of Irish unionism came its religious leaders as the Church of Ireland Primate, the Presbyterian Moderator and the Methodist President added their signatures. By the end of the day 237,368 men had signed the Covenant, while 234,046 women had signed the broadly similar Declaration.

The idea of a public covenant drawing together religious and political convictions was not new. Covenanting had a long history in the Scottish Protestant tradition and at first the inclination of those organising Ulster's opposition to Home Rule was to modify the text of an existing Scottish Covenant. In the end, however, a completely original document was drawn up. The Covenant read:

> *Being convinced in our consciences that Home Rule would be disastrous to the material well-being of Ulster as well as the whole of Ireland, subversive of our civil and religious freedom, destructive of our citizenship, and perilous to the unity of the Empire, we, whose names are underwritten, men of Ulster, loyal subjects of*

His Gracious Majesty King George V, humbly relying on the God whom our fathers in days of stress and trial confidently trusted, do hereby pledge ourselves in solemn Covenant throughout this our time of threatened calamity to stand by one another in defending for ourselves and our children our cherished position of equal citizenship in the United Kingdom, and in using all means which may be found necessary to defeat the present conspiracy to set up a Home Rule Parliament in Ireland. And in the vent of such a Parliament being forced upon us we further solemnly and mutually pledge ourselves to refuse to recognise its authority. In sure confidence that God will defend the right we hereto subscribe our names. And further, we individually declare that we have not already signed this Covenant. God save the King.

On the surface this Covenant, unlike those of the Scottish Covenanters, appears to be a purely political statement with little content that could be described as theological. This could create the impression that the theological and religious significance of the events was not central. However, this is to overlook the context in which the Covenant was drawn up.

Ulster Protestants did not need to have the significance of religious belief for political life explained to them - they understood it perfectly well. Nor must the Covenant be detached from the wider events of the day of its signing. Ulster Day was a religious event. The leaders of Irish Protestantism and the ordinary men and women in the pews signed the Covenant together. Those of a liberal religious disposition stood side by side with those of a conservative religious disposition and sang 'O God our help in ages past.' It was precisely because of this intimate connection between religious identity and political identity that unionist people of all political and denominational persuasions did not need to be persuaded of its salience.

On Ulster Day, Protestant churches and the Protestant community were indistinguishable. The cause of true religion and the cause of Ulster unionism ran in perfect harmony.

Home Rule - The Issues

The arguments against Home Rule were repeated from public platforms, in parliament, in books, pamphlets and newspapers throughout the years of crisis. What is noticeable is the consistency of these arguments throughout the period. While there may have been differences of emphasis and nuance depending on the speaker and the audience the overall thrust of unionist objections comes across clearly.

First, Home Rule posed a religious threat:

> *The contention of the Irish Protestants is that neither their will nor their religious liberties would be safe in the custody of Rome. In an Irish parliament civil allegiance to the Holy See would be the test of membership, and would make every Roman Catholic member a civil servant of the Vatican. That parliament would be compelled to carry out the behests of the Church. The Church…claims to be above Civil Law, and the right to enforce Canon Law wherever she is able.*[12]

Against a background of Catholic renewal in Ireland, Catholic involvement in the Home Rule movement and a more conservative move in Catholicism generally, Protestants could see nothing but harm arising from an arrangement that left Catholicism as the dominant power in the land. Catholicism was held to be fundamentally anti-Protestant. Catholicism was also viewed as essentially illiberal in its social and educational values. Protestants feared a new ascendancy of Catholicism which would impose this religious and social illiberalism on the whole of Ireland. Thus when Protestants said Home Rule is Rome Rule they believed it.

Nor was concern over the role of Catholicism restricted to those on the more conservative edges of Protestantism. Presbyterian liberals, having only recently been freed from the illiberalism of one established church, had no desire to return to a new form of establishment under Catholicism. This was an issue that united both liberals and conservatives in both religion and politics within unionism.

Second, unionists argued on the simple basis that they were not part of the Irish nation but that they were part of the British nation:

> [Ulster Protestant] ideals are the ideals of the whole British nation. They are not Irish in that sense and England and Scotland form part of their ideals. Their ideals are Imperial ideals...[W]e regard the term Briton as the emblem of liberty. We have prospered under it and we will take nothing less. And instead of the sentimental humbug about Ireland's well-being...we maintain our own ideals because we are connected with Britain by ties of blood...religion and history; and we object to being swallowed up in the claim that...we should come into [Redmond's] fold because we live in Ireland.[13]

But more than this, Ulster Protestant identity was bound up not just with Britishness but with Empire - the greatest, wealthiest Empire the world had ever known. Ulster Protestants had helped to build this Empire and had benefited from it, not least in the industrialisation of the North East and the Lagan Valley in particular:

> We hear a great deal of the false sentiment of Ireland a nation...We Ulstermen also have a sentiment, but it is a pride in the greatness of British Imperial citizenship - pride in the share we have taken in peace and war, in science and art, in Government and colonisation, in everything that went to the building of this Empire - pride in the memory of great deeds done by our forefathers.[14]

A third line of argument concerned the threat posed by Home Rule to the economic well being of Ulster and Belfast in particular. The difference between industrialised and progressive Belfast and the agrarian and backward state of the rest of Ireland was marked, and Ulster Protestant knew why:

> Under the Union every industry in Ulster and Belfast especially is flourishing; but what industry has flourished in the South and West of Ireland, unless it be moonlighting, boycotting, agitation, resisting the law and crime?[15]

48

Home Rule it was believed would lead to the running of this great industrial city being placed in the hands of farmers and economic incompetents. Belfast's wealth would be used to prop up a rotten economy. Separated from the wealth and stability of Empire, Belfast's industries would never be able to raise capital to maintain their progress.

Finally, Ulster Protestants also argued against Home Rule on the basis of their understanding of the constitution. The key point they stressed was that no government had the authority to forcibly expel citizens against their will:

> *Unionists hold...that their claim to remain under...the Imperial Parliament is an inalienable right of their citizenship which no Government of any time has the right to deprive them of. There need be no mistake about this, it is the position which Ulster has taken up all along; it is the heart and the essence of what has come to be called the Ulster Question.*[16]

Nor was this considered an obscure or unusual argument. Bonar Law, leader of the Conservative Party, Lord McNaghten, Lord of Appeal, and AV Dicey, the greatest constitutional theorist of that time, all advanced this argument.

The objections to Home Rule, then, were multiple in nature. It is not proper to adopt a reductionist approach. Such approaches were not uncommon either then or now. For some, unionist objections could be reduced to religious bigotry - and were, therefore, not to be discussed but to be faced down. Thus the liberal politician, the Earl of Crewe, asserted that the only sentiment involved in Ulster unionism was "that of hatred to the Church of Rome."[17] And Augustine Birrell, the Liberal Chief Secretary for Ireland, claimed in 1913 that "the pulse of the [Ulster unionist] machine is religious bigotry."[18]

On the other hand, some Home Rulers reduced unionist objections to economic concerns alone, believing that guarantees could be provided that would ease their fears. Such an approach failed to recognise the reality of unionist religious concerns and the strength of the sense of British and Imperial identity among unionists.

This failure to appreciate the strength of religious convictions in the unionist position - a failure common to many contemporary analysts as we shall see - was doubly mistaken. For as well as recognising the multi-causal nature of unionist opposition to Home Rule, it is important to recognise the interrelationship between these causes. These were not separate and discrete arguments; they were intimately connected - though in some cases the connection is more obvious than in others.

One of the less obvious connections is the way that a religious worldview informs all of these arguments. After all, as we have seen, Britain's sense of its Imperial power and economic success was intimately linked to Britain's sense of itself as a Protestant nation. And Britain's constitution and the liberties and freedoms deriving from it were a political manifestation of Protestantism. Hence the construction of Britishness with which Ulster unionists identified had, at its core, a religious - more specifically - a Protestant worldview, which interpreted both its past and its present in religious terms.

This is not to reduce all opposition to Home Rule to religious matters only. It is to insist on the pervasive influence of a religiously informed view of political and social reality underpinning and informing the multi-causal objections to Home Rule. It is to insist that religious belief cannot be pushed to the margins nor can it be reduced to a mere set of private beliefs and practices which do not impinge on 'real' issues of politics, social order and economics.

This multi-causal nature of unionist opposition to Home Rule and the role that religion played in it, can be brought into sharper focus through a brief study of the life and work of one of unionism's key thinkers and organisers, Thomas Sinclair.

Thomas Sinclair[19]

If Henry Cooke represented evangelical religion and conservative politics, Sinclair embodied evangelical religion and liberal politics. In this he was perhaps truer to his non-conformist tradition, for in British political life non-conformists tended to see liberal politics as a progressive force compatible with their own agenda.

However, Sinclair's liberalism did not make him any less hostile to Home Rule. For Sinclair's opposition to Home Rule was driven precisely by his liberal convictions. Sinclair was strongly and consistently opposed to the establishment of religion in any form by the state. Thus, unlike Cooke, he favoured disestablishment of the Church of Ireland. For Sinclair, the true bulwarks against the encroachments of Catholicism and nationalism were business, liberal political policies on land reform and equal citizenship rights for all.

A further consequence of his convictions was his opposition to what he viewed as a potential Catholic ascendancy under a Home Rule parliament. Even before Home Rule became the key issue in Irish politics, Sinclair was campaigning against state endowment of Catholic education. Once Home Rule took centre stage, Sinclair's considerable energies and abilities were channelled into its defeat.

It was Sinclair who played a leading role in organising the Great Convention of 1892 which brought together all strands of Unionism to declare their opposition to Home Rule. And it was Sinclair who organised the Presbyterian anti-Home Rule rally in 1912. It was Sinclair who wrote newspaper articles, who addressed rallies in Ireland and Scotland, who organised businessmen and politicians against Home Rule, who made representations to business and political leaders in England and who shaped debates in the Presbyterian General Assembly. Above all, it was Sinclair who drafted that defining expression of Ulster's opposition to Home Rule, the Solemn League and Covenant.

Sinclair was no religious extremist, no sectarian fanatic. Yet Sinclair as much as anyone argued that Home Rule was Rome Rule. For Sinclair the Empire and Britain stood for all that was progressive, enlightened and liberating, while Catholicism stood for social control, impoverishment and religious establishment.

Sinclair could not see how a Home Rule parliament with a majority of Catholic members could escape the pressure to reshape Irish society in the image of a Catholic state - even if that was not their intention. Ulster's wealth, Ulster's freedom and Ulster's liberties could not survive under such a regime. Thus for Sinclair, "it was his belief that he was being steadfast in his liberal principles which often occasioned his most strident warnings about Home Rule and Catholic power."[20]

Yet, as we have seen, this did not make Sinclair unique or even unusual. Rather, it simply demonstrated the extent to which Sinclair was one with nonconformist liberalism throughout Britain in the late nineteenth century. Sinclair was a British liberal as much as an Ulster unionist.

CONCLUSION

In this chapter we have tried to show the religious background to Irish politics in the nineteenth century, and, in particular, the religious dimension to unionism's opposition to Home Rule. However, we have also tried to show that there is no aspect of unionism's attitude to Home Rule and its religious implications that is not perfectly understandable within the wider British context.

Nineteenth-century Irish unionists were also nineteenth century British citizens. They shared the Empire Protestantism of their fellow citizens. The difference lay simply in the context in which that citizenship was lived out. In Ireland it was lived out against the background of a numerically stronger and increasingly powerful Catholic Church and community. As a consequence, elements of the British Protestant tradition, which had faded from view in England retained their currency - or were sharpened in their focus - in Ireland.

3

KEEPING THE FAITH

Religion and 'The Troubles'

INTRODUCTION

Clearly there was a time when religion mattered deeply in both Britain and Ireland. This religion was not simply a set of private beliefs with no public relevance. Rather, this religion had interpretive power as men and women tried to make sense of their past and their present. Moreover, this religion also had the power to shape political decision making.

This is not to say that the worldview of earlier generations of Britons and Irish people was shaped only by religion to the exclusion of all else. It is to say, however, that it is impossible fully to understand the past of Britain and Ireland without taking seriously the influence of religion on belief and practice – both in private and in public.

However, even if this is accepted, the obvious question that arises is whether religion still plays this significant role, or must we see it exclusively as an historical phenomenon. More specifically, we need to ask if religion still has interpretive power for communities in Northern Ireland as they reflect on and respond to the political and communal conflict.

INTERPRETING NORTHERN IRELAND

The Irrelevance of Religion

Judging from much of the academic literature on Northern Ireland it would seem that religion plays little part. Social scientists in particular seem to see little sign of the social and political significance of religion. So two standard surveys of approaches to the interpretation of the Northern Ireland situation both minimise the role of religion.

John Whyte, in his *Interpreting Northern Ireland*,[1] has an extensive survey of literature which deals with the role of religion in maintaining segregation but notes that "segregation by itself does not necessarily make for conflict." Segregation, rather, "can…exacerbate conflict…in a situation where other reasons for conflict exist."[2] The question that this raises is whether religion itself can be a cause of the conflict. Whyte uses the answer to this question as "a thread through the maze of differing interpretations."[3] Having surveyed a cross section of the literature on the conflict, Whyte concludes that "to extreme evangelical Protestants, the conflict is primarily religious: they see the struggle as one between Christ and Antichrist. To a much wider spectrum of Protestants, the conflict is religious in the sense used by Bruce, of religion as being a badge of identity."[4]

While at first glance this might seem a reasoned and reasonable conclusion it is, in fact, deeply flawed because of the attenuated concept of religion that Whyte is working with. A conflict is religious, Whyte seems to suggest, if "the antagonists are contending about religious doctrines or interests."[5] He will allow that on a different definition of religion - one that sees it as a badge of identity – it may be appropriate to see the conflict more strongly in religious terms. However, this definition Whyte describes as "peculiar."[6] Yet it is nothing of the sort. As we have seen, Protestant objections to Home Rule were rarely pitched in terms of competing doctrinal claims, yet it is clear that they derived from a broader religious interpretation.

Similarly, for contemporary Protestants 'religion' is about more than a set of beliefs. Religion has implications for the whole of one's political, social, economic, cultural and personal life. It is this broad interpretation of religion that is normative within religious communities and it is the interpretation of religion that sees it only as dealing with "religious doctrines or interests" that is, in fact, "peculiar." However, this reduction of religion to a set of beliefs and interests and the failure to see how religion functions in communities to shape identity and worldview is not unique to Whyte. It is, rather, pervasive throughout much of the literature on Northern Ireland.

The second work is John McGarry and Brendan O'Leary's *Explaining Northern Ireland*.[7] They deal with religious interpretations of the conflict in a chapter entitled 'Warring Gods? Theological Tales'. Their conclusion, having surveyed a broad range of material including some works that appeared after the publication of Whyte's book, is that "explanations which emphasize the primacy of religion...need to be exposed to strong light. When that happens, they evaporate, leaving little residue."[8]

However, this decisive conclusion is premised on highly dubious analysis. To mention only two of the difficulties: first, McGarry and O'Leary's approach is reductionist in the extreme and, second, like many other works, it is based on an understanding of religion that owes more to sociological theory than it does to the self-understanding of religious communities.

Repeatedly throughout the relevant chapter McGarry and O'Leary suggest that if the conflict is about religion then it cannot be about anything else. "If [those who place religion at the heart of the conflict] are right, important implications follow. Socio-economic inequalities, cultural or national differences, inter-state relations, and political institutions must be of secondary or no importance. The conflict must be pre-modern, with essentially endogenous roots. Policy implications also follow: 'religious' solutions have to be canvassed such as secularization, ecumenism, or integrated education."[9] Or again, "If the antagonisms are religious, then they cannot have been caused by the historic legacies of colonial conquest plantation, and oppression, by the Stormont regime's practice of political and economic discrimination against nationalists, by successive British governments' mismanagement in Ireland before and after 1972, or by British political institutions."[10]

The deep flaws in this kind of thinking should be obvious. In the first instance, even taking for the sake of argument the overly restrictive concept of religion that McGarry and O'Leary are using, no one has claimed that the conflict is exclusively religious. Second, just because a conflict is religious it does not mean that the conflict is not also economic, or cultural, or political. Since McGarry and O'Leary themselves emphasise the "multiple nature of the divisions between the two communities,"[11] it seems strange that they cannot find room for any meaningful role for religion in their analysis.

However, the greater difficulty with this analysis is, once again, its failure to understand fully the nature of religion. McGarry and O'Leary suggest that since communities in Northern Ireland do not describe their perceptions of the conflict in 'religious' terms it cannot be a religious conflict.[12] Thus for McGarry and O'Leary, if politicians and people in Northern Ireland do not constantly justify their actions and demands with reference to religious beliefs then this is evidence that their concerns are not religious. And because loyalist paramilitaries "generally shun overtly religious targets"[13] like "unarmed priests and nuns,"[14] clearly they are not motivated by religion.

McGarry and O'Leary, when discussing Protestant attitudes stress the cultural and economic reasons for Protestant opposition to a united Ireland. "These fears," they argue, "are sufficient to explain…why so many Protestants are unwilling to accommodate nationalists."[15] The implication seems to be that economic and cultural attitudes can be explained apart from any reference to religion.

At the heart of the problem lies the inability of many social scientists to comprehend the nature of religious belief and its social significance. As we have seen, just because a unionist opponent of Home Rule was talking about economics it did not follow that religion was irrelevant to the argument, for economics and religion were intimately linked. The continued existence of a community for whom religious belief is capable of shaping economic, social and political attitudes confuses many social scientists because it refuses to fit in with either their experience or their theories.

Social scientists are taught to believe that religion constitutes a set of private beliefs and practices that do not and cannot impinge on the public sphere. Moreover, they inhabit an intellectual universe where this is indeed the case. However, the imposition of this model in relation to the religious community in Northern Ireland demonstrates a failure of intellectual imagination and intellectual laziness in their reluctance or unwillingness to take religiously defined worldviews seriously. The end result is that their writings often tell us more about the ideological convictions of secular social scientists than they do about the people of Northern Ireland.

The Centrality of Religion

Of those social scientists and historians who do take seriously the significance of religion in the conflict the best known is Steve Bruce.[16] In his most recent work on Northern Ireland Bruce argues that two groups – paramilitaries and evangelicals – "can lay claim to vital symbols of Ulster unionism and can exert considerable influence on Protestants beyond their own numbers because they articulate and act out responses which, to a greater or lesser extent, are found in almost all unionists. They do not typify unionism, but they exemplify, in extreme form, beliefs and values that in weaker versions are held by most unionists."[17]

Bruce's assertion of the importance of conservative Protestant religion[18] for the wider unionist community is based on a more sophisticated understanding of the nature of religion than is usual among social scientists. "Religious ideas and images," he suggests, "influence the way people think and feel; they can structure relationships between groups. Religions readily becomes involved in social conflict because they help people make sense of their circumstances and they help to justify them."[19]

So, while Bruce rejects the idea that all unionists interpret the conflict in terms of a struggle between God and the devil, between Protestantism and Rome, his point is that evangelical religion is a core constituent of the ethnic identity of Ulster loyalists. Evangelicalism resonates with Ulster loyalists far beyond those who would define themselves as evangelicals because, argues Bruce, "[evangelicalism] defines the group to which he belongs, it figures large in the history of that group, it legitimates the goup's advantages (such as they are), and it radically distinguishes the group from its traditional enemy."[20]

While recognising that "the connections between religion and politics are not easy to untangle and they certainly cannot be meaningfully reduced to a simple link between evangelical piety and conservative unionism," Bruce's assertion is that "evangelicalism, by virtue of its place in the history of the Irish conflict, has become the core of ethnic identity, the guarantor of the ethnic group, and that, from that position, it impinges strongly, albeit subtly, on the responses of a large number of apparently secular Protestants."[21]

For Bruce, then, the Protestants of Northern Ireland form one ethnic group which is in conflict with a national group, and at the heart of the Protestant ethnic identity is evangelicalism. Thus the conflict is an ethnic conflict in which religion plays a significant role.

A different approach is taken by the historian Donald Akenson.[22] Akenson explores three communities – the Afrikaners, Ulster-Scots and Israelis – through the lens of the biblical concept of covenant. Akenson discovered as he examined these communities that "what they had in common was their understanding of how the world worked. And that understanding stemmed directly from the Hebrew scriptures."[23] Having outlined the shape of the covenant, Akenson concludes that "these societies will not be given to easy compromises, committed to religious or racial pluralism, or overly concerned about keeping the good opinion of the outside, profane world. To keep the deal that is the covenant, a society must be uncompromising, adamantine, self-contained."[24]

Akenson traces the development of the covenantal culture in Ireland through the theological influence of Calvinism and the political influence of Scottish covenanting culture. The Presbyterian settlers of the North East of Ireland were shaped by these twin influences. Akenson suggests that the covenantal culture of Presbyterianism then became diffused throughout the wider Protestant population in the nineteenth century as a result of the increasingly close relationship between the Presbyterian Church and the Church of Ireland and of the rise of evangelicalism.

While acknowledging the reality of social change on this society, Akenson suggests that "the Ulster-Scots conceptual grid had more effect upon modernization than the other way around – in the sense that instead of the Ulster-Scots mindset being forced into the conceptual outlook of the modern industrial world, the Ulster-Scots were able to subordinate most of the complex changes involved in the modernization process to their own conceptual system."[25]

The covenantal culture of Ulster Protestantism was embodied in the state of Northern Ireland and maintained until the late 1960's. Since then, argues Akenson, the covenant has been coming apart.[26] "Protestants in Ulster no longer belong to a single covenantal culture," he claims.[27] Having lost control of the levers of political power in the early 1970's Protestants found they could not rely on their alternative bulwark, the churches, since many of the clergy and leaders of these churches had themselves abandoned the covenantal culture. The result has been that the covenantal culture of Ulster Protestantism has been fragmenting, both politically and religiously.

Yet, as Akenson realises, these fragments are not insubstantial and are highly volatile. "It will take more than a single generation," he concludes, "for them to cool down and during the waiting period, a miscue by British, Irish or European authorities could make them coalesce once again."[28] Conservative Protestantism may no longer be the defining reality in Irish unionism, but its apparent loss of influence at the public level should not lead the observer to conclude that it no longer matters.

Conservative Protestantism and the Belfast Agreement

As an illustration of the continuing political influence of conservative Protestant belief we can look at some of the debates within the unionist community during the period between the signing of the Agreement on April 10 1998 and the subsequent referendum.

Throughout the talks process that culminated in the Agreement the received wisdom was that the greatest potential stumbling block for unionism concerned the creation of political structures institutionalising the relationship between Northern Ireland and the Republic of Ireland – that is, North-South structures. It was feared that many in the Protestant community would reject any set of structures that appeared to undermine the effectiveness of new political structures within Northern Ireland or that appeared to be a mere transitional stage to a united Ireland.

However, following publication of the Agreement there was little discussion of the proposed North-South structures, or, for that matter of any of the proposed political structures. Instead, in the Protestant community, public debate - and public anger - was focused on the proposed early release from prison of convicted members of terrorist organisations. It would be easy to suggest that this debate was driven by anger, by bitterness, by personal suffering or by factional interest. It would be easy - but it would be foolish. In fact, there was - and remains - a deep-seated conviction among many in the Protestant community that this aspect of the Agreement is unjust.

More than this, there were some who on pragmatic grounds would have voted for the Agreement in the subsequent referendum, but who, on the basis of moral opposition to the release of prisoners, either voted against it or did not vote. The primary reason why many in the Protestant community felt and feel so strongly about this matter is that their understanding both of the nature of justice and of the role of Government is significantly shaped by a worldview framed by conservative Protestant religious beliefs.[29]

Some of these beliefs are:

1. The chief purpose of Government, as the biblical writer Paul outlines in his letter to the Romans, is to punish evildoers. Justice, as Protestantism has traditionally understood it, is primarily about crime and punishment. So a Government that in pursuit of political agreement releases prisoners is setting aside its God-given responsibility to govern.

2. The role of Government, according to Paul in the same writing, simply reflects the role of God himself. Protestantism has stressed that God makes himself known as a God of justice. And this justice cannot simply be set aside as and when it suits God to do so. The commitment to justice defines the way God must act if he is to be true to himself.

So God may choose to forgive human beings but in doing so he must act in a way that is consistent with justice. Thus Protestantism stresses the judicial aspects of the death of Christ - Jesus is punished, Jesus bears God's wrath, the demands of justice are met, human beings are declared righteous and so on. So if God, to be true to himself, cannot set aside the demands of justice, who are we, who are politicians, to do so?

3. Finally, we also need to remember the importance of the theological category of covenant within the conservative Protestant tradition. Covenants, of course, have a legal dimension. The requirements of the covenant are given in laws. Obedience to the law results in blessing; disobedience results in punishment.

These theological convictions are conveyed in the multitude of sermons, hymns and liturgies of conservative Protestantism. This is especially true in relation to the second of these convictions. Hymns, prayers and sermons constantly remind churchgoers of the judicial dimension of Christ's death and the Christian's salvation.

While it is true that patterns of religious affiliation are changing in Northern Ireland it remains the case that levels of churchgoing are extremely high, and that they are yet higher among those who would identify themselves as theologically conservative. Even among those who do not attend church themselves it is quite common for them to send their children to events and meetings for children organised by local churches - particularly in rural areas.

Bear in mind, too, that if levels of church-going are high now they were higher still in the past. Bear in mind the conservative Protestant chaplains of Orange Lodges who take every opportunity to explain conservative Protestant beliefs to their non-church going fellow members. Bear in mind the high profile leaders within the Protestant community who combine unionist politics with conservative Protestant religion. Ian Paisley is only the latest in a long line of such people.

The consequence of all this is that, both directly and indirectly, conservative Protestant beliefs continue to have a key role in shaping how Protestants in general think and act. Public opposition to the political process premised on explicitly religious grounds was not uncommon during the referendum campaign.

So, a brief trawl through the website of the Democratic Unionist Party[30] - a Party that strongly opposes the current political process - turns up a great many references to "the representatives of unrepentant terrorists." The same phrasing can be found on the website of the ostensibly secular United Kingdom Unionist Party.[31] Many of those in the more mainstream Ulster Unionist Party who oppose the process are themselves practising Christians of a conservative Protestant kind.

At the time of the referendum a group calling itself *Christians Against the Agreement* put advertisements in newspapers and published materials condemning the process as violating Christian principles. One such advertisement was entitled 'The Sin of Voting Yes.'[32] Another, discussing the release of prisoners, was headed, 'Christ or Barabbas?'[33] The Orange Order, an organisation heavily influence by conservative Protestantism, formally declared itself against the process during the referendum campaign.

This is not to argue that any Protestant opponent of the release of prisoners asked to explain his or her opposition would recite this list of theological convictions. However, it is to argue that these convictions shape and inform attitudes and values within the Protestant community.

It was these deeply held convictions shaped by religious belief that very nearly stopped the current process in its tracks in the referendum and the subsequent elections to the Assembly. True, a majority of unionists voted for the Agreement and a majority of those unionists returned to the Assembly are pro-Agreement, but in both cases the majorities are slim. Moreover, despite apparent progress in the process over the past months, the concerns of many in the Protestant community have not gone away. We would suggest that it is foolish for social scientists or policy makers to ignore the extent or depth of the convictions that give rise to these concerns in the Protestant community.

CONCLUSION

Clearly, we cannot resolve this dispute among social and political scientists and historians. However, it is worth noting the increasing rejection of a reductionist mentality which dismisses the significance of religion, especially among historians.[34]

Authors like Bruce and Akenson argue academically what many conservative Protestants know instinctively - that conservative Protestantism has a significance for the Protestant community in Northern Ireland that extends beyond the four walls of the churches where it is preached.

Yet, even if this were not the case, the numerical strength of the conservative Protestant community and its role in the political and social life of the community would make it essential for anyone who wanted to understand the nature of the wider community to understand and respond to this tradition.

Of course it might be more comfortable to hope that the power and influence of religion will gradually be eroded by social change. Politicians, social scientists and others would undoubtedly be happier analysing and dealing with a secular society in which religion was nothing more than a private affair of the heart. However, there are a number of difficulties with this scenario.

First, it is not likely to happen in the immediate future – how long are they prepared to wait?

Second, it is not clear that it will happen at all. The eminently modern United States stands as a challenge to all convenient theories of secularization. While the United States is a modern society its very pluralism creates an environment in which religion – specifically conservative Protestant religion –thrives. And this conservative Protestant religion thrives, moreover, on engagment with the public sphere.[35] Northern Ireland may go the way of secular European countries, but what if it follows a different, American, model?

Finally, this approach is based on the arrogant assumption that religion in the public sphere can only be a bad thing, and ignores – consciously or otherwise – the power of religion to contribute to the resolution of conflict and to peace-making in a society in conflict.[36]

It has been argued in this chapter that conservative Protestant religion is still of significance for a considerable section of the community in Northern Ireland, still formative for Protestantism beyond those who practice a form of conservative Protestant religion, and will remain for the foreseeable future a key constituent of life and society in Northern Ireland.[37]

Given this, it is imperative to understand something of the beliefs and values of this tradition as they impinge on issues of politics and society, belonging and identity in Northern Ireland. In the next section conservative Protestant perspectives on three crucial themes - God, land and nation - will be assessed.

PART 2

4

EVERYTHING LOOKS DIFFERENT

Self, Society and the Triune God

ENVISIONING GOD

The Bible presents us with a series of images of God. God is holy, loving, gracious, just and forgiving. God is father, lord, king, judge, shepherd, friend, healer, saviour, keeper, defender. God is a rock, shelter, support, tower, sun shield, rampart. God is a lion and a lamb. God is light. God is mysterious, but God is among us. Thus Christians are not short of images for God from within the Biblical tradition. And when we add in the New Testament dimensions of God made known in Christ and God coming in the Spirit we have yet more scope for envisioning God.

Yet our image of God is never merely an intellectual construct, nor a pious formulation contained within the bounds of the church. For Christians, God is - to use some more images - all in all; God is lord and creator of, not only the individual, but of individuals who relate socially. Consequently, for men and women and, in particular, for societies where a Christian vision of God has been a central aspect of their self-understanding, these images of God have impinged directly on our image of society.

And this is not just society understood as a collection of individuals or families. Nor is it solely the Christian society of the church. For these images of God have significantly impinged on the construction of society as a political body. "Subtle connections are made and conclusions drawn as a result of the analogy – sometimes explicit, frequently implicit – between God and the state. A people's image of God affects political behaviour and conceptions of civil authority influence religious behaviour. Ideas and assumptions about the nature of authority in one sphere necessarily affect beliefs and actions in the other."[1] It is worth bearing in mind just how many of the most common images of God have political dimensions - Lord, King, Ruler, Judge.

However, the relationship between our vision of God and our vision of society works both ways. It is not only our vision of God that impinges on our vision of society, for our vision of society also impinges on our vision of God. So, for example, a person brought up in a high-church tradition will have a different vision of God from a person brought up in a charismatic tradition. Equally, a person brought up in a secure middle class home in a Western liberal democracy will have a different vision of God from someone brought up in poverty under a totalitarian regime.

Of course, these are not two mutually exclusive ways of constructing the relationship between the image of God and the image of society. In reality it is a two-way street; our vision of God impinges on our vision of the world and our vision of the world impinges on our vision of God. This, of course is how it should be. Christians claim that God is Lord and Creator of all things, that he remains engaged with his creation and that he has a plan for the future of our world. Thus a Christianity that did not connect the image of God with the image of society would be sadly lacking. Nevertheless, just because there should be a connection between these two visions, it does not follow that every connection made within the Christian tradition should be accepted as legitimate. Connecting the vision of God and the vision of society can distort both visions.

This raises the question of whether any particular Christian tradition has adequately or fully expressed the relationship between these two visions in a way that does justice to both? More specifically, has the conservative Protestant tradition with its stress on the authority of the Bible been able to construct the relationship between the image of God and the image of society in a way that avoids the dangers of distorting both? For if this tradition has such an understanding then it can claim to have a crucial grasp of how society should be shaped as well as how God should be understood.

On the other hand, if this tradition suffers from the same difficulties as other Christian traditions in this area, then conservative Protestants too must be willing to abandon flawed understandings of the relationship between God and society. And they must go further in looking afresh at the image of God and society in order to better express and enact the relationship between them.

CONSERVATIVE PROTESTANTISM AND THE VISION OF GOD

This tradition does not have a single defining image of God. Nor do conservative Protestants have a single defining image of society. Whatever the key characteristics of this tradition might be, these are not among them. In fact, conservative Protestants hold to a wide diversity of views on both matters, though certain images of God and society have been more commonly found than others.

However, there are two images of God that have played a significant role within the conservative Protestant tradition. On the one hand, the image of God as a God who enters into covenants is central to the self-understanding of the Reformed tradition. In Ireland the centrality of the Reformed tradition meant that this covenantal theology also became part of the self-understanding of the wider Protestant community. The second image is of God as a God of justice whose justice is most clearly expressed in the death of Jesus Christ.

The Covenant-Keeping God

Clearly, the image of God as a God who enters into a covenant with his people is foundational in the Bible. God's covenantal relationship with Abraham promises nationhood and blessing. Abraham's descendants will constitute a 'great nation' who will inhabit a clearly-defined land (Genesis12.12; 15.18-21), and through this nation God will bless the nations of the earth (Genesis 12.3; 22.15-18). However, alongside the promise was the demand for obedience (Genesis 17.1; 18.18-19).

The book of Exodus tells the story of the covenant God made with his people at Sinai as the promises made to Abraham began to reach their fulfilment. Israel had indeed become a great nation and God had brought them out of captivity and was bringing them towards the land promised to them. The covenant, reiterating the promises of God to the people he has chosen also sets out a new challenge to them as they take possession of the land (Exodus 19.3-6). The Ten Commandments (Exodus 20.1-17), the Book of the Covenant (Exodus

21-23) and the sacrificial and other regulations set out in the book of Leviticus all serve the one purpose of enabling the people to live in the land in conformity with the will of God, thus fulfilling their calling to be a witness to the nations and the means of their blessing.

However, while God's commitment to the covenant and his purpose of blessing through the covenant is absolute and assured, this is not to say that the people can ignore the obligations that their partnership in the covenant lays upon them. For disobedience will bring judgement even as obedience brings blessing (Leviticus 18.24-28; Deuteronomy 30.11-20). One final important covenant is that made with David (2 Samuel 7). Again, God makes promises to David and his descendants and places them under obligation to obey God's commands.

The biblical covenants present a consistent pattern. God's initiative and grace in establishing the covenant are stressed. But demands are made of those to whom God is gracious. These demands are all embracing, defining human relationships with God, with other people and with the rest of the creation. They also govern the relationship of the people with one another. Yet these demands are not intended as a burden on humanity. They are, rather, made in order to enable Israel to live as God intended, to flourish in its own national life and to bear witness to the graciousness of Israel's God.

As a social and political entity the covenantal community of Israel exists in relation to core questions of nationality, of identity and of relationship to other nations. The people of Israel were familiar with the idea of territorial gods who ruled a particular piece of earth and who were worshipped by the inhabitants of that territory. Israel, too, stressed the territorial rule of God without ever conceding that the God of Israel was anything less than the ruler of the whole of the creation (Exodus 19.4-6). The Bible also emphasised that God had first chosen Israel and then gifted them a land. Both the choice of a people and of a territory reflected the freedom and sovereignty of Israel's God. Thus the covenant brought into intimate relationship God, land and nation.[2]

The constant reiteration of the need for obedience makes clear just what a radical challenge was being set for the people and, indeed, much of the story of Israel is the story of the people's failure to rise to the challenge. Repeatedly the prophets call Israel to account for their failure to honour the covenant. Their worship is a half-hearted performance of rituals, their social and political relationships are marked by lies, corruption and exploitation. Far from being a light to the nations Israel is often at best indistinguishable from the nations, at worst excelling the nations in wickedness (Ezekiel 5.6-7; Micah 3.9-11; 6.6-8; Amos 2.4-8; 4.4-5; 5.21-25).

Consequently, when the patience of God runs out and the people do not return to him, judgement falls. The devastation of exile comes upon the people and they are expelled from the land of promise. Yet the covenant remains and the Old Testament story of Israel ends with the return to the land.

In many ways Israel learned the lesson of exile and, despite the failings of the people following the return to the land, Jesus came to a people with a strong sense of their own distinctness and a determination to maintain their separation from the contamination of other nations and other gods. In particular, the Pharisees strove to maintain the purity of Israel through observance of the law and strict separation, not only from non-Jews but also from those Jews who had failed to maintain the required level of purity. Any other course was perceived as threatening Israel's distinctiveness and, therefore, Israel's mission in the world.

"In the circumstances which confronted Israel," – of a land occupied and corrupted by the presence of Gentiles – "the importance of the law for Israel's self-understanding as the covenant people of God was bound to come to focus in those elements of the law which brought their sense of distinctiveness and separateness to most explicit and visible expression and which thus functioned for good or ill as test cases of loyalty to the covenant people and to God."[3] The Pharisees pursued a noble aspiration – an Israel faithful to the covenant and faithful to the law in the land God had given them. Yet their practice

79

built barriers between Jews and Gentiles and between the Jewish people. Israel, far from being a light to the nations, was turning its back on the nations, stressing its difference from the nations in order to survive. It was in danger of becoming an introverted, defensive community – not holy, just strange.

This too represented a failure to keep the covenant. The true purpose of the covenant – the flourishing of God's people and their witness to the nations - had been lost in the quest for purity. Hence Jesus in his encounters with the Pharisees and others challenged them in their understanding of the covenant and its implications for how they lived. Whether through laxity or zeal, the purpose and role of the covenant in God's plan for his people had been thwarted.

This is the obvious and ever-present danger of the covenantal concept: human beings lose sight of the origins of the covenant in the grace of God, and the purpose of the covenant in human flourishing in relation to God and witness to others, focussing instead on the covenant's demands. This corruption of the covenant results in a religion which stresses rule keeping as the primary mode of faithfulness. As the emphasis on the rules comes to dominate, there is a need to expand the definition of the rules or add subsidiary rules to cover circumstances not covered in the biblical text itself. The end result is a religion that talks of grace but lives by law, and a God who is primarily a rule-maker and rule-enforcer.

A nation that so misunderstands the notion of covenant is immensely vulnerable to both complacency and pride. Complacency arises when a community believes that God has a special relationship with them, and conclude that they are immune from divine judgement. Pride arises when this presumed special relationship leads the community to look down on or exclude those who are not part of the community and so not part of the relationship. The covenant is no longer open to others but closed and protected against others. Those who do not belong are no longer welcomed as strangers and aliens but subjected to suspicion, hostility, even violence. The boundaries of the community are drawn ever more strictly. Those who are deemed to be covenant breakers find themselves expelled.

What is true of the human community is true also of the physical space the people inhabit. Survival in the land becomes increasingly dependent on maintaining purity through obedience to the rules. Impurity - whether of the covenant breaker or the alien - threatens, and so both must be expelled, or pushed to the margins.

The covenant, given as a gracious gift by God for the well-being not only of the people of the covenant but for the whole of God's world, is a fundamental theological category. However, the covenant easily becomes defensive, suspicious, inward looking when God's people lose sight of the grace that defines the covenant.

The God who Does Justice

The Bible constantly speaks of justice, righteousness and judgement. God is a God of justice (Deuteronomy 32.4; Psalm 94.2; Malachi 2.17) and God's will is that human society be administered justly. To that end God's people are given a law covering all aspects of their life together and in relationship with God. In doing justice, human beings are to reflect the justice of God himself (Leviticus 18.4; Deuteronomy 1.17).

Ultimately, the law is about setting things to right and so ensuring that society is ordered on the principle of equity. The covenant itself, with its complex regulations of social life and its promises of blessing and warnings of judgement reflect this emphasis on God as a God of justice. Within the conservative Protestant tradition, the idea of the justice of God is most clearly focused through that tradition's understanding of the death of Christ.

Substitutionary Atonement

The conservative Protestant tradition has long been committed to what is known as the penal substitutionary theory of Christ's death.[4] The logic of the argument is relatively straightforward. All human beings have broken God's law and are therefore guilty and deserve to be punished. However, God sends Jesus to take the place of human beings. In his death he takes upon himself the penalty owing to human beings for their sinfulness. If human beings repent and put their faith in Jesus they are forgiven and declared just by virtue of Jesus' death. This teaching has its roots in biblical tradition, was formulated afresh in the satisfaction theory of Anselm in the eleventh century and received its classical Protestant shape in the major Confessions of the Protestant churches.

Biblically, the broad sweep of both Old Testament and New is a story of fall and salvation. Humans are alienated from God as a result of their faithlessness and rebellion – they are sinful. God's purpose is the restoration of humanity to a proper relationship with him. But this requires that some means be found of dealing with human sinfulness – that is, how sin may be atoned for. In the Old Testament the means by which atonement is made and sinfulness overcome is a complex system of sacrifices (Leviticus 9.7).

Though some Christian traditions tend to play down the significance of God's wrath against sin, it nonetheless represents a major biblical theme. In particular God's wrath is focused on rebellious humanity (Romans 1.18,24,26,28; Ephesians 5.6; Hebrews 10.26-31; Revelation 19.11-21). However, the just punishment that human beings deserve as a result of their sin falls instead on Jesus Christ in his death. There is a penalty for sin which Jesus has paid (Romans 3.25-26; 6.23; Galatians 3.13) by dying in the place of sinful human beings (2 Corinthians 5.21; 1 Peter 2.24).

While this interpretation does not exhaust the biblical exploration of atonement, sacrifice and Christ's death, it is nonetheless a significant strand within it and one that tends to dominate the thinking of conservative Protestantism. So, the major Protestant Confessions systematise these biblical elements in their portrayal of the atonement. Both the Westminster Confession of Faith - the doctrinal standard for the

Presbyterian Church – (*Chapters VI.vi; VIII.v; XI.i-iii*) and the Thirty Nine Articles of the Anglican Communion (*XI; XXXI*) clearly teach this doctrine.

This model, then, is not simply something to be found in theological textbooks or discussion of theology among the enlightened. This model forms the confessional and teaching core of the conservative Protestant tradition. It is taught to those who profess faith in order to help them understand their faith. It is preached to those who do not profess faith in order to persuade them of their need to do so.

It is also proclaimed in the popular hymnology of conservative Protestantism – a point whose significance should not be overlooked. For, as Mark Noll has commented, "The classic evangelical hymns…contain the clearest, the most memorable, the most cohesive, and the most widely repeated expressions of what it means to be an evangelical."[5]

In particular, the classic hymnody of Protestantism emphasises the demands of justice and Christ's satisfaction of those demands. Examples from the hymns of some of the best known Protestant hymn writers abound, and these can only hint at the pervasive presence of this theology throughout the canon of Protestant hymnody.[6]

The Role of the State

Nor is this the end of the matter. The judicial imagery of Christ's death allied to the covenantal model already creates a powerful set of ideas. However, these are reinforced yet further through the conservative Protestant emphasis on the role of the state. While there is a wide range of biblical material that directly or indirectly addresses the nature and role of the state and the Church's relationship to the state, conservative Protestants have tended to focus on one key text from Paul's letter to the church in Rome:

> *Everyone must submit himself to the governing authorities, for there is no authority except that which God has established. The authorities that exist have been established by God. Consequently,*

83

he who rebels against the authority is rebelling against what God has instituted, and those who do so will bring judgement on themselves. For rulers hold no terror for those who do right, but for those who do wrong. Do you want to be free from fear of the one in authority? Then do what is right and he will commend you. For he is God's servant to do you good. But if you do wrong, be afraid, for he does not bear the sword for nothing. He is God's servant, an agent of wrath to bring punishment on the wrongdoer. Therefore, it is necessary to submit to the authorities, not only because of possible punishment but also because of conscience. Romans 13.1-5

The conservative Protestant reading of this passage stresses the responsibility of the state to exercise justice by punishing those who do evil. Hence, the primary function of the state is judicial. That this text has become the key text on the role of the state within this tradition is unsurprising given its emphasis on the judicial nature of God's dealings with humanity. Thus these interpretations of the covenant, the death of Jesus and the role of the state are mutually interpreting and mutually reinforcing.

Implications

The social implications of this vision of God are clear. True religion involves conformity to rules. Moreover, these rules not only govern relationships within the church and between Christians but also between the church and the wider community, and within the wider society and its political structures. It is in keeping the rules that justice is to be found, and in punishing rule-breakers that justice is to be maintained. Because these rules are given or are held to derive from the Bible, they are not negotiable, bearing as they do the hallmarks of divine order and justice. Thus compromise, negotiation and accommodation are not mechanisms for social well-being but constitute declension, sell-out, treachery.

Failure to maintain the rules, moreover, is not just a matter of personal disobedience, for the covenantal model stresses the wider social implications of that failure. The covenant promises blessing for obedience but punishment for disobedience. Thus the failure of some impinges on the well-being of all, for it brings the punishment of God on all.

The covenant model, allied to the interpretation of the role of the state as primarily an agent for the punishment of evil, also legitimises political opposition. If the state is seen to be failing in its God-given responsibilities, if the state fails to keep to the rules, then the state too comes under the judgement of God. If the state is perceived to promote evil, or even fail to act against it, then the state may be resisted.

Consequently, this vision of God can lead to considerable suspicion of any political, social or religious change. Any change that is interpreted as undermining the social and political models generated by this vision is not merely change, it is disobedience and, as such, to be resisted.

This kind of thinking is most clearly associated in Northern Ireland with organisations like the Free Presbyterian Church and the Orange Order. But, as we have seen, these kinds of ideas are common to the foundational documents of both major Protestant traditions in Northern Ireland and are equally commonly found among smaller Protestant denominations.

The obvious question that arises at this point is, given the dominance of these themes in the broader conservativeProtestant tradition why have the same kinds of perspectives that exist within this community in Northern Ireland not arisen among similar groups elsewhere? The answer is that indeed they have.

Timothy Gorringe argues that the judicial metaphors of Christ's death powerfully shaped political and social thinking in eighteenth and nineteenth century England.[7] Likewise, the idea of covenant as a religiopolitical metaphor for interpreting the nature of state and society is not uncommon, especially in those societies influenced by a Presbyterian tradition. Hutchinson and Lehmann note the widespread appropriation of the covenantal concept of chosenness in societies influenced by Christian tradition.[8] But why have these theological models and images retained their ability to shape perception in Northern Ireland when it seems clear that in most other contexts they have been translated into secular visions with the religious component becoming increasingly marginal?

Akenson's comparative work on South Africa, Israel and Ulster provides a partial answer.[9] What the Afrikaaners, Jews and Protestants have in common is that they are all communities that perceive themselves to be under threat. Thus while the other, whose presence helps define the limits of the community and provides the justification for stressing the need for covenant faithfulness, remains a reality the covenant model will not simply fade away.

Another part of the answer is the continued significance of the form of conservative Protestantism known as evangelicalism. As we have seen, evangelicalism provided a powerful means of uniting Protestantism and separating it from Catholicism. That this evangelicalism was mediated through the Presbyterian tradition means that the concept of covenant was privileged.

The continuing sense of being a community under threat, allied to a still significant evangelicalism combines with the theological imagery of covenant and substitutionary atonement to create a community in which the image of God conveyed by this theology powerfully defines the community's image of itself and its obligations.

It is all too easy to dismiss these kinds of beliefs as of no consequence. However, this vision of God shapes the way many conservative Protestants interpret the history of Northern Ireland, which in turn shapes political perspectives within the unionist tradition, defines social movements such as Orangeism, supplies the content of much church teaching and influences voting patterns in elections and referendums. This vision is, in fact, internally coherent, deeply resilient and strongly held. To ignore it is to miss the point behind much Protestant thinking, talking and acting.

Conservative Protestantism, then, like other Christian traditions, has been shaped in its view of family, society, church and politics by its view of God. Similarly, its view of family, society, church and politics has shaped its view of God. Whether the shaping has been true to God or not, whether it has contributed to the well-being of society or not - these are the crucial questions.

In passing it should be noted that this is not the only way in which the image of God impinges on the image of society within the Protestant tradition in Northern Ireland. There is also a more liberal theological and political tradition. This tradition stresses God's love and compassion. Theirs is the God of reconciliation and dialogue. This tradition, wittingly or otherwise, draws on another dimension of Presbyterian thinking - the transformative dimension of God's work in the world - including the transformation of societies. This tradition tends to be more at ease with liberal societies, viewing them in effect as the fullest expressions of God's aspirations for society. Thus, this tradition, as much as any other, endorses the status quo.

In the light of this the crucial question is this: Are there alternative images of God and society that can help us deal with these issues? The conservative Protestant tradition itself may have no distinctive answers to give, but as part of a broader Christian tradition there are two key areas where conservative Protestants could find a new vision of God and a new vision of society that would not be an endorsement of anybody's status quo.

The first of these lies in a rediscovery of the doctrine of the Trinity as a meaningful way of knowing God and responding to God - rather than a simple assertion we make doctrinally. This rediscovered Trinitarianism is not just about mentioning the work of Father Son and Holy Spirit and affirming their equality. It is about reflecting on the very being of God and asking what that has to say to us in our being human. This brings us to the second area. The connection between the being of God and our human being is important and valid for one simple, biblical, reason. We are, all of us, made in God's image. We are most fully what God wishes us to be when we bear that image most clearly.

THE TRINITY – DOGMA OR DOXOLOGY

Conservative Protestants confess, with other Christian traditions, God as Father, Son and Holy Spirit. However, when it comes to the expression of that belief in hymnology or proclamation what is noticeable is the thinness of Trinitarian reflection. This is not to say that the Trinity is ignored. Father, Son and Holy Spirit are ever-present in the worship and preaching of this tradition.

However, they are present in a rather functional manner which emphasises the acts of Father, Son and Holy Spirit; more specifically their acts 'for us' in salvation. There is little sustained reflection on the relationships of Father, Son and Spirit with each other as God. Where there is, the emphasis tends to be on the Father and Son relationship, but again this tends to focus on the relationship as it is 'for us' rather than as it is in itself.

Trinitarian thinking, therefore, tends to take place in the context of thinking about other aspects of Christian theology. Rarely is the Trinity considered central to our understanding of these other doctrines, and rarer still is it considered central to our public theology or political theology. Yet the confession of God as Father, Son and Holy Spirit is foundational for Christianity. The doctrine of the Trinity "is neither an appendix nor a prolegomenon to theology but the apex and goal of theology."[10] However, neither our preaching, nor our worship nor our discipleship would suggest that this is so.

Instead, Christian faith and practice has largely been shaped by what is distinctive confessionally rather than what is shared. These distinctive elements are at the core of each tradition's understanding of Christianity, not only in disputes with other traditions but in internal reflection on the Christian faith also. As a result, Trintiarianism is professed as a dogma but rarely defines our doxology. As Colin Gunton has it, "the Trinity has more often been presented as a dogma to be believed rather than as the living focus of life and thought." The challenge, Gunton goes on to suggest, is to make the Trinity that living focus since "everything looks different in the light of the Trinity."[11]

If this is so, then the question raised is, How different do ideas about God – the God of the covenant and the God of justice – land and nation look in the light of the Trinity? However, before turning to that issue some further reflection on the Trinity is required.

Understanding and Misunderstanding the Trinity

One of the difficulties many Christians have with the Trinity is the strangeness of Trinitarian language. What does it mean to speak of 'one substance' and 'three persons'? What is the difference between communicable and incommunicable attributes? Between essence and energies? Between generation and procession?

Unfortunately, the inadequacies of human language for God can often cause difficulties for the understanding of God. The phrase, 'one substance in three persons' is an example of this. The difficulties are two-fold. On the one hand the language might seem to suggest that there is somehow 'behind' the three persons – Father, Son and Spirit – a more fundamental reality – the one substance – which is God. Consequently, the one substance becomes more crucial, the persons less so.

On the other hand the language of 'person' tends to convey to contemporary men and women the idea of an individual with his or her own will and discrete identity. Consequently, the persons – understood as discrete individuals - become more crucial, while the persons in their unity and mutual indwelling become less so. These, of course, are not new problems, but our distance from the intellectual and psychological world of the church fathers who developed this language makes it even more of a challenge for contemporary men and women.

One of the ways early church writers tried to complement this technical language was to develop a series of analogies. Many were tried but the best known and most sustained and most influential attempt at finding an appropriate analogy was Augustine's psychological analogy. Augustine compared God as Father, Son and Spirit with the human person as being, knowing and willing. Developing this model in relation to human psychology, he spoke of the mind, its knowledge of itself and its love for itself. Bringing human psychology into relationship with God he developed his analogy further by speaking of the mind as remembering God, knowing God and loving God.[12]

This analogy, whatever its merits, suffers from one great flaw. By basing his analogy on the human individual, Augustine emphasises the unity and oneness of God at the expense of the relational nature of God as Father, Son and Holy Spirit. The end result once more is that the distinctions between the persons and their mutual relations become secondary.

The language of Trinitarian theology, of course, does not claim to define or reveal God. The church fathers were well aware of the pitiful inadequacy of their language as they tried to speak of God, yet the task was important for Trinitarian doctrine was worked out in the face of assaults on the Christian gospel from heretical teachers. For modern Christians, the inevitable inadequacy of language for God is compounded by its distance from us and its consequent strangeness. A recovery is required; a recovery that not only brings to life the language we know but that perhaps brings a renewed emphasis on aspects of Trinitarian thought that, for different reasons, have never become as central to Trinitarian thinking.

A Relational God

One of those aspects is that which emphasises the centrality of the relationships between the persons of the Trinity. God is a community in himself. The Father, Son and Holy Spirit are not simply descriptions of how God is made known to us but are a description of the essential nature of God. Before the world was made God existed as Father, Son and Holy Spirit in relationship. This relationship has been described in Christian theology as one of mutual indwelling (John 10.38). That is, they are not distinct to the point of separation. The Son is a distinct person, but he is the Son only because the Father and the Spirit also indwell him. So also with the other Trinitarian persons. Consequently, to see the Son is to see the Father (John 14.9-10).

This mutual indwelling is not marginal or derivative but is at the very heart of the Christian understanding of God. God is, in his very being, relational. "There is in God genuine diversity as well as true unity. The Christian God is not just a unit but a union, not just a unity but a community. There is in God something analogous to 'society'. He is not a single person, loving himself alone, nor a self-contained monad or 'The One'. He is triunity: three equal persons, each one dwelling in the other two by virtue of an unceasing movement of mutual love."[13]

This mutual indwelling, however, does not simply describe a static and abstract relationship. At the heart of this relationship, as Ware notes, is mutual love, for, as John insists, God is love, and whoever lives in love lives in God and God in him (1 John 4.7-21). Despite the trivialisation of John's words, not least by Christians, they take us to the heart of God. "The unity of God is nothing less than the self-dedication of the trinitarian persons to each other. Indeed, God is love – the divine essence is the love that binds together the Trinity."[14]

It is with this perspective on the Trinity in mind that we turn to the second of the two key areas that can give us a fresh orientation on our thinking about the relationship between God and society.

MADE IN THE IMAGE OF GOD

While the idea of humanity as made in the image of God is limited to a few texts in the Old Testament,[15] these texts have always occupied an important place in Christian thinking about human identity. That this language was taken up by New Testament writers and given a christological focus only enhances its importance.

There have been a number of interpretations of the meaning of the image. There is a long tradition going back to the early church which interprets the image as humanity's bearing of certain distinctive characteristics, usually moral and rational abilities. This is often linked to an approach which differentiates the 'image' from the 'likeness' with the former identifying qualities that are retained after the fall and the latter referring to those aspects of humanity that were lost.

The Reformers rejected the distinction between image and likeness taking them as synonyms. They also rejected the view that the image consisted of natural human qualities. Instead they viewed the image as reflecting the relationship between God and humanity before the fall. This relationship - sometimes referred to as original righteousness - was destroyed by the fall. However, the reformers also interpreted the image dynamically: what has been lost can be restored through Christ. The image is the reality toward which human beings are moving.

A third approach sees the image as indicating humanity's role as God's representative on earth. Adam and Eve are given the task of subduing the earth and ruling over the rest of creation. A fourth interpretation emphasises the significance of creation of humanity, male and female, as God's image and focuses on the relational capacity of human brings.

The sparseness of references to the divine image in the rest of the Old Testament makes it extremely difficult to determine where the truth lies among these various interpretations. What does seem reasonably clear is that the distinction between image and likeness is no longer credible. Consequently, to identify the image with rational capacity seems questionable since the result is that the fall of humanity makes no difference to humanity's being in God's image. It seem then that the remaining three approaches which emphasis an original relationship now destroyed, a mandate to rule over creation as God's representative, and a relational capacity, all have merit.

It is, however, the latter that we want to focus on and bring into relation with the understanding of the Trinity noted above. This is how Colin Gunton expresses it:

> *If, first, to be created in the image of God is to be made male and female, what is implied is that in this most central of all human relatedness is to be found a finite echo of the relatedness of Father, Son and Holy Spirit. To be God, according to the doctrine of the Trinity, is to be persons in relation: to be God only as a communion of being. It is that which is replicated, at the finite level, by the polarity of male and female: to be in the image of God is to be called to a relatedness-in-otherness that echoes the eternal relatedness-in-otherness of Father, Son and Spirit.*[16]

The implications for our understanding of what it means to bear the image of God in our relationships with one another as church, as neighbours, as political community require exploration. But before we turn to that we need to consider Jesus Christ who, in his person, lives the perfect communion of the Trinity and manifests the divine image perfectly.

JESUS CHRIST
SON OF GOD - IMAGE OF GOD

The language of the image reappears in the New Testament. The clearest reference to Genesis 1.26-27 appears in the letter of James: *With the tongue we praise our Lord and Father, and with it we curse men, who have been made in God's likeness* (3.9). However, the most significant appropriation of this language is found in Paul's letters where it is given a Christological significance.

For Paul, Jesus Christ is the supreme bearer of the divine image: *The god of this age has blinded the minds of unbelievers, so that they cannot see the light of the gospel of the glory of Christ, who is the image of God* (2 Corinthians 4.4). And he bears this image, not only as the revealer of the gospel, but as the creator and sustainer of the universe: *He is the image of the invisible God, the firstborn over all creation. For by him all things were created: things in heaven and on earth, visible and invisible, whether thrones or powers or rulers or authorities; all things were created by him and for him. He is before all things, and in him all things hold together.* (Colossians 1.15-17).

For human beings - with our relationships with God, other humans and the rest of creation corrupted by sin - the way to true humanity is found in the transformation of our lives so that they too bear the divine image once more. It is God's purpose, asserts Paul in his letter to the Romans, that Christians *be conformed to the likeness of his Son* (Romans 8.29). However, this is a gradual process of transformation: the Christians at Colossa, says Paul, *have put on the new self, which is being renewed in knowledge in the image of its Creator* (Colossians 3.10). Similarly, to those in the city of Corinth he writes: *And we, who with unveiled faces all reflect the Lord's glory, are being transformed into his likeness with ever-increasing glory, which comes from the Lord, who is the Spirit.* (2 Corinthians 3.18). However, this transformation into the divine image is the ultimate goal of human salvation and is assured by God himself: *And just as we have borne the likeness of the earthly man, so shall we bear the likeness of the man from heaven* (1 Corinthians 15.49).

Jesus Christ, then, is the true image, the model of true humanity. If we are to understand what it means to bear the image of God it is to Christ that we look. But Jesus Christ reveals to us not only human life in all its fullness but the life of God. John's gospel in particular reveals to us the inter Trinitarian relationships between Father, Son and Spirit. The mutual love and mutual indwelling that we noted above are common themes throughout John (John 1.18; 10.34; 12.44; 14.6-11; 17.10, 21).

Jesus Christ reveals to us the relationships that lie at the heart of God and the relationships that mark true human being. Jesus Christ is not only Saviour, but revealer – of God and of our humanity – and model. Jesus Christ, as he reveals to us the Trinitarian life and mission, is the measure by which our understanding of Christian theology must be judged.

We are made in the image of God, made for relationship with God and one another uncorrupted by fallenness. Yet, given our fallenness, all such relationships can only ever be echoes of the reality and require that we give ourselves to their outworking constantly. Instead of the self-giving and open relationality of Father, Son and Spirit, fallen human beings resist relationship, refuse to allow relationship to constitute their identity and seek to overcome or deny the other. As Christians we have absorbed uncritically the contemporary idolatry of the self as "the notion of the self as subjective consciousness [has] displaced the centrality of mutual participation, both in the doctrine of God and in the Christian understanding of human community."[17]

"The outcome," asserts Cunningham, "is visible all around us; in its glorification of the isolated individual, our culture is profoundly antitrinitarian. At every level, through practically every system and structure, we are discouraged from allowing our lives to become too tightly intertwined with those of others."[18]

And what is true of our fractured personal relationships is true also of our fractured social and political relationships, for even where we do manage to form relationships of political community, social class or denominational allegiance, rarely are these open to others who do not 'belong'. The idolatry of the self can encompass not only the individual but also the group. And corresponding to the idolatry of the self there is the demonisation of the other.

But this is not the Christian way. "Made after the image of God the Trinity, human beings are called to reproduce on earth the mystery of mutual love that the Trinity lives in heaven…Each social unit…is to be made an ikon of the Triunity."[19]

5

THIS OTHER EDEN

Belonging, Identity and Place

Land matters. Not just land in general, or any old piece of land, but 'our' land - the land of our birth, the land we have worked and shaped, the land, perhaps, we have fought to defend.

Human beings need to belong, to be rooted. Land is still important. In the West we have become, in many respects, rootless people.[1] Yet for most of the world's men and women land - and particular pieces of land - remain central to their belonging and identity. Many live and work on land handed down from generation to generation. Life and death, joy and sadness, fear and hope are shaped and bounded by this land. Exile from the land - whether chosen or imposed - remains for many men and women a tragedy, for exile from the land is exile from belonging, identity, home.

In the West this intensity of belonging to a particular piece of land remains important in rural and agricultural communities but less so for the rest of us. We are people who have a degree of mobility unknown to earlier generations and still unknown to many men and women around the world. Yet while we may travel far from home, still there is always a home to which we return or of which we dream in our wandering. Or, if return is not possible we attempt to put down new roots, to find a new belonging, to be anchored.

In the West, too, we have heightened our collective sense of belonging to the land through our emphasis on the nation, bringing the two into intimate relationship. "National identity," suggests Simon Schama, "would lose much of its ferocious enchantment without the mystique of a particular landscape tradition: its typography mapped, elaborated, and enriched as homeland."[2]

Our land is often a place of battles - of victories and defeats. Our land has its holy places - churches, yes, but also those places, natural and created, that are icons of our identity. Our land is celebrated: it is 'green and pleasant'; it is 'beautiful for spacious skies'. Our land is sacred too because it opens up to receive the bodies of its sons and daughters, its heroes and champions. Its soldiers who die in other lands are gathered together in and buried in plots that become 'our' land. Our land, because it is ours, becomes worthy of the sacrifice of the lives of men and women, and so the land in turn becomes more precious because their blood has been spilled.

And if we struggle to express our bond to the land, our pride and our belonging, our poets will provide us with a liturgy:

> *This other Eden, demi-paradise,*
> *This fortress built by nature for herself*
> *Against infection and the hand of war,*
> *This happy breed of men, this little world,*
> *This precious stone set in the silver sea...* Richard II 2.1

Yet here lies the danger of the land – of our land. If our land is Eden, then other lands must be east of Eden – a place of exile and of curse; a place inhabited by those driven from the presence of God and bearing the mark of Cain. Our land must be preserved, protected against all that threatens – whether immigrants, asylum seekers, foreign powers and their armies. Our land must not be corrupted, its purity sullied, the paradise lost, the fortress breached, the silver sea parted.

The land is more than simply the theatre of our lives, it is an integral part of our lives; it shapes us, defines us, makes us who we are as peoples and communities. Our land, the gift of God, the place of our flourishing, becomes our god and our idol, becomes a place where only pride and hostility can flourish.

Land, then, is a deeply ambiguous symbol. On the one hand, the promise of land is central to God's fulfilment of his plans. The land, blessed by the presence of God can, indeed, become a holy land. On the other hand, land becomes an idol, an end in itself. No longer valued as the sphere of God's activity, it becomes the defining icon of identity - an identity intimately dependent on the survival and flourishing of that land.

Conservative Protestants have no particular theology of the land. Consequently, they lack the resources necessary to challenge views of the land that sacralise 'our' space while demonising the other. They, too, identify with the symbols and stories of conquest, creativity and sacrifice that invest the land with a meaning far beyond mere geography. Yet, without a coherent theoology of the land they have no capacity to develop a critique of this point of view.

However, while conservative Protestants have no particluar theology of the land, nonetheless, their understanding of the land can be influenced by biblical perspectives. This is perhaps especially true for those Protestants whose theological tradition focuses on the idea of convenant. This biblical influence is more clearly seen with reference to the idea of the nation, or the community. But, to the extent that communities or nations are embodied or expressed in territory, the Bible exerts a secondary influence on thinking about the land.

The rest of this chapter aims to set out the framework for a Christian theology of the land. We will look first at the significance of land in the story of Israel, identifying a number of perspectives on land. Then we will look at the reinterpretation of land in the ministry of Jesus and the apostles. Finally, we will reflect on the implications of the broad biblical perspective for our life as community in the land where God has placed us.

LAND IN THE OLD TESTAMENT[3]

Land as Gift

When God came to Abram, he called him to leave his country (12.1). The identity, security and belonging of place were to be surrendered voluntarily in obedience to God. Yet Abram's pilgrim wanderings came with the promise of a new land, a new home (12.1-8). It was this promise of place that sustained Abram in his journey and, later, sustained the people of Israel in their Sinai pilgrimage. God was the God of the whole earth, but God's people were to be gifted a very particular part of that earth.

Israel's land is neither owned nor taken, but given. The land, like the whole earth, belongs neither to Israel nor to the earlier inhabitants of the land Israel conquered or displaced, but to God. Nor is this gift of land merely an act of divine generosity. It is, rather, an integral and crucial aspect of the covenant that God entered into with Abraham. As the covenant is initiated, confirmed and reconfirmed the promise of the land remains central: *To your offspring I will give this land* (Genesis 12.6); *To your descendants I will give this land* (Genesis 15.18); *The whole land of Caanan...I will give as an everlasting possession* (Genesis 17.8). The covenant also links the gift of land with the promise of offspring - the promise that Abraham will become a great nation (Genesis 12.2; 15.5; 17.4-6). Clearly, then, at the heart of Abraham's relationship with God are these twin themes of land and nation.

More than gift, though, the land is also Israel's inheritance (Deuteronomy 12.9,10; 31.7; Psalm 105.9-11). An inheritance is given from a parent to a child and, as such, identifying the land as Israel's inheritance asserts the strongly relational dimension of the gift. Israel is God's child; God is Israel's father. Along with the gift comes the certainty of God's care and provision for his people.

Land as Task

The land was given to Israel in order that Israel might live in obedience to God, embodying in its life a godly vision of community. Through living in obedient relationship to God, Abraham and his descendants would know the blessing of God and would themselves be the means by which God would extend that blessing to the nations (Genesis 12.1-3).

That godly vision came to Israel as yet another gift from God. In the Torah, given through Moses at Sinai, God set out for the people the pattern of godly living, not only in relation to the worship of God, but also in their life together as a people and in their relationships with the strangers among them and the neighbours - and enemies - on their borders. The gift of Torah enabled Israel to live as a godly community, a faithful community, both politically and socially. Thus the land as task challenged Israel to embody in all aspects of its life as a nation the vision gifted to it at Sinai. It was only as Israel responded in obedience to this gift that they would experience the blessing of God and be the means of blessing to the nations, for possession of the land without obedience to the law would leave the godly vision unfulfilled. As Brueggemann notes, "The land as a social reality, that is, not simply as a piece of real estate, takes on a different quality, depending upon the attitude, conduct, and policies of its inhabitants. Places depend upon the kind of people who inhabit them and take on the character of their occupants."[4]

Land as Temptation

As the giver of land and law, God was not indifferent to the attitude, conduct and policies of the people of Israel as they attempted to embody the godly vision in the land. Israel may have been in possession of the land, but God was still the owner of the land and the God of the people. Yet Israel was often tempted; tempted to focus on the gift, to find their purpose, their security and their hope in the land rather than in the God who gave them the land; tempted to abandon the godly vision for society and politics given in the law to follow instead the godless visions of their neighbours. Israel was often tempted to believe that by playing by the rules of its neigbours it was more likely to survive among its neighbours.

Yet the irony was that by accommodating itself to this godless vision Israel was simply making itself more vulnerable. At one level the nation was vulnerable to its more powerful neighbours. Alliances were made and remade, but when the ally fell, Israel fell too. Philistines, Assyrians, Babylonians, Egyptians, Romans and others at one time or another shattered Israel's peace and laid waste the land. However, the point of Israel's greatest vulnerability was in the people's relationship with their God who kept his covenant even when the nation forgot it or broke it.

And Israel often forgot the covenant or broke the covenant. Israel's history was a history of failure, followed by divine critique through God's prophets, followed by restoration and renewal. Often, however, restoration was preceded by punishment, for Israel did not heed the divine critique and the nation found itself captive in its own land or exiled in a strange land. For every Josiah *who turned to the Lord...with all his heart and with all his soul and with all his strength* (2 Kings 23.25) there was a Manasseh w*ho did evil in the sight of the Lord* (1 Kings 21.2). Consequently, while the people knew much of the blessing of God, often they knew more of his punishment. Yet, ultimately, God's commitment to his covenant and his purpose of blessing for the nations meant that even the threat of exile came with the promise of restoration (Jeremiah 29.10).

Land as Holy

In the Old Testament holiness has a physicality that is strange to us. The presence of God in a place makes that place holy. Because God was in the land, the very land itself was holy. At the centre of the land was the holy city - Jerusalem. At the centre of Jerusalem stood the Temple. And at the heart of the Temple was the Holy of Holies - the place where God dwelt.

That the holy God was present among the people of Israel and, by his presence, giving holiness to the land itself meant that it was imperative that both the people of Israel and the land remain pure and undefiled. So, for example, God's complaint against his people spoken through Jeremiah is that they have polluted the land: ...*you came and defiled my land, and made my inheritance detestable* (Jeremiah 2.7). The holiness of the land had been sullied because Israel had compromised its relationship with the true God by pursuing false gods (Jeremiah 3.10). Corrupt and corrupting social practices had the same effect: abusing and exploiting the poor, the widow, the orphan and the alien profaned the holiness of the land (Jeremiah 2.34; 5.20-31; 7.1-34). Israel's practice of contracting military and political alliances with foreign powers was another source of impurity (Jeremiah 2.13-19). The consequences of Israel's pollution of the land were invasion, destruction and exile (Jeremiah 52.12-19). Trusting in the presence of God in his Temple for their security (Jeremiah 7.4) the people deceived themselves.

Israel's return from exile witnessed a determined systematic programme under Ezra and Nehemiah to restore the sacred space. Those religious and social practices that threatened the purity of the land were tackled head on: the economic abuse of the poor by the wealthy was denounced; Sabbath observance was vigorously advocated; intermarriage was condemned. Separatist social and religious practices were necessary if the land were to be holy and unpolluted, acceptable to God.

Land as Home

Each of the previous perspectives on land tends to treat the land in an abstract manner. However, for those who made their home on the land, the men and women, the families and tribes of Israel, the land was no mere abstraction. Even as gift, even as holy place, the land remains primarily home. The land in the bigger sense is important, but the people of Israel relate to the land through the little patch of land that is home. It is here that children are born, sons and daughters wed and parents die and are buried. It is here that houses are built, fields cultivated, and livestock reared. It is here - in the patch of land that is home - that Israel's people remember their joys and sorrows, their memories and regrets.

In exile the people knew Babylon only as a 'strange place' where they tilled an alien soil and wept bitter tears for home - Zion:

By the rivers of Babylon we sat and wept
when we remembered Zion.
There on the poplars
we hung our harps,
for there our captors asked us for songs,
our tormentors demanded songs of joy;
they said, "Sing us one of the songs of Zion!"
How can we sing the songs of the LORD
while in a foreign land?
If I forget you, O Jerusalem,
may my right hand forget its skill.

*May my tongue cling to the roof of my mouth
if I do not remember you,
if I do not consider Jerusalem
my highest joy.*

Psalm 137.1-6

This rootedness, this belonging to the land, is clearly part of God's design for his people and for all people. As human beings we are rooted in this earth. God made us from its dust and placed humanity in a particular plot of this earth - the garden of Eden (Genesis 2.15). Eden was a place of identity, security and belonging. The price of humanity's rebellion was exile from the garden (Genesis 3.23). For Cain, too, the price of his violence was exclusion from the land he had tilled and a life of wandering (Genesis 4.11-14). Cain could make his home anywhere (Genesis 4.16), but anywhere was not home. Home was a memory of another place, a place Cain could return to no more.

God's law also emphasises the importance of belonging by ensuring that those among his people who are dispossessed will, ultimately, recover the land and the homes that were theirs (Leviticus 25.10,28,40). The prophets, too, denounce those among the wealthy of Israel who pursue their own well-being at the expense of those poorer and weaker than themselves (Isaiah 5.8; Amos 2.6-7; 4.1). To leave their neigbours without home or land is to sin against God. Poor and rich alike need to be rooted in the land, need to be at home in the land.

Land, then, is central to the Old Testament. Whether as gift, as task, as temptation, as holy space or as home, this theme crops up repeatedly in these texts. The question then is, how do the New Testament writers approach the theme of land?

LAND IN THE NEW TESTAMENT[5]

The New Testament has surprisingly little to say directly about the land given its significance in the Old Testament and its central role in the covenantal promises. However, the silence of the New Testament and the indirect reflection on the theology of the land are important.

Jesus and the Land

Jesus spoke little about the land but had a great deal to say about the role of the Jerusalem Temple and the purity laws. Both of these were intimately related to Israel's understanding of the land as holy. As noted above the holiness of the land was focused in the Temple and, most of all, in the Holy of Holies. The purity laws ensured that the people of Israel remained undefiled and would not contaminate the land. At a time when Israel was a subject people, the integrity of the Temple and the purity of the righteous became all the more important, hence the intensity of the conflict in precisely these areas between Jesus and his opponents.

All four gospels record the incident in the Temple (Matthew 21.12-17; Mark 11.15-18; Luke 19.45-46; John 2.13-22). While traditionally referred to as the cleansing of the Temple, there is good reason to believe that it was, primarily, an acted prophecy of its destruction. So both Matthew and Mark place the story of the fig tree in close attendance to the Temple story (Matthew 21.18-20; Mark 11.12-14). The point is clear – Jesus came seeking fruitfulness but, finding none, the consequence was judgment and destruction. Elsewhere Jesus speaks clearly of the destruction of the Temple (Mark 13.2) and of the city of Jerusalem (Luke 19.43-44; 21.20-24).

The precise meaning and implications of Jesus words and actions in relation to the Temple do not concern us here. What is clear, however, is that Jesus was calling into question the centrality of the Temple for Israel's covenantal relationship with God. If the Temple was no longer the focus of holiness, then the very idea of Israel as a holy land was being called into question.

As a consequence of calling into question the relationship between holiness and the land, Jesus was also calling into question the purpose of the purity laws and raising anew the question of what it meant to pursue holiness and resist defilement. The purity laws practiced by Jesus' opponents were intended to safeguard their holiness and so the holiness of the land. However, it was not only things that could cause defilement but people also. As a result the effect of the purity laws was to establish boundaries between those who observed them and those who did not.

Jesus' refusal to be restricted by those boundaries was a constant source of conflict. He was repeatedly accused of meeting with and eating with sinners – those who were unclean (Matthew 11.19; Mark 2.16; Luke 15.2; 19.7). On one occasion, when Jesus' disciples were criticized for eating with unclean hands Jesus gave his definitive statement on the matter: *Listen to me, everyone, and understand this. Nothing outside a man can make him 'unclean' by going into him. Rather, it is what comes out of a man that makes him 'unclean.'* (Mark 7.14-15). No longer circumscribed by the boundaries of ritual purity, Jesus touched and was touched by those who were unclean. The result was not as his critics imagined. Instead of his holiness being contaminated, his holiness drove out the defilement (Mark 5.1-20; Luke 8.43-48). Again, the precise implications of this need not concern us here. But Jesus' response to the practice of ritual purity laws reinforces what we saw in relation to the Temple – namely, that holiness was no longer to be understood in relation to a specific territory – the land - which needed protection against defilement.

So, if Jesus teaching was calling into question the centrality of the land, what was he offering in its place? At the heart of Jesus' ministry was his announcement of the coming of the Kingdom of God. Old Testament anticipations of the Kingdom saw in its coming the restoration of creation, a restoration that would be marked by the healing of sickness (Isaiah 35.1-3, 5-6, 10). The coming king would overthrow evil and bring the exile of the nation to an end (Isaiah 52.7-10). Jesus, the coming king, intended his ministry and his mighty deeds to be seen in this light. Thus when John the Baptist questioned Jesus' ministry, Jesus responded by pointing to his healing ministry as the sign of the coming of the Kingdom (Matthew 11.4-6). The implication of Jesus' identification of himself in this way is that Israel, while living in the physical land of Israel, was not yet restored and was still, in fact, in exile (Nehemiah 9.36). It was the life, death and resurrection of Jesus that constituted the fulfillment of the promise of Israel's restoration, not a return to the land. Thus the hopes of Israel's righteous, of Anna, Simeon and Zechariah, were fulfilled not in a material sense but in the person and ministry of Jesus. Israel's Kingdom had been restored through Israel's King, Jesus, but his Kingdom was not the Kingdom of Israel but rather the Kingdom of God.

It seems then that Jesus in his words and deeds challenges the deepest convictions of the people of Israel concerning the role of Jerusalem and the Temple. By implication, Jesus is also challenging the traditional view of the land. Yet this should hardly come as a surprise. Jesus' ministry provoked the hostility of many precisely because he radically redefined core aspects of Israel's sense of identity and belonging. The Sabbath, food laws, relationships with non-Jews - all were challenged, shaken, redefined by Jesus in word and deed. The king had come, but few in Israel could understand the implications, few were able to face up to the new challenges Jesus presented.

Paul and the Land

Like Jesus, Paul has little to say about the land directly. However, looking at the wider context of Paul's thought it becomes clear that there are major implications for the theology of the land.

Galatians 3.6-29

In this passage Paul discusses at length God's covenant with Abraham. No mention is made of the promised land; instead Paul's focus is on the promise that all the nations will be blessed (v 7-9,14,27-29). Moreover, the source of this blessing is Jesus Christ, the true offspring of Abraham (v 16). So the promise made to Abraham is of blessing for Jews and Gentiles alike who through faith are in Christ. *And if you are Christ's*, says Paul, *then you are Abraham's offspring, heirs according to the promise* (v 29; see also Romans 4.1-25 and 8.15-17). The promise of land has thus been radically reinterpreted.

Colossians 1.12-14

This passage may not, at first glance, seem pertinent to this theme. But the clue lies in Paul's use of the idea of inheritance. As we have noted, the Old Testament used the language of inheritance to express the gift of the land within the framework of the relationship between God and Israel.

Now, however, the inheritance that is given to God's people takes on a new dimension. God's people have been *rescued for the dominion of darkness and brought into the Kingdom of the Son he loves* (v 13-14). Here we have an echo of Israel's experience of liberation from Egypt and the journey towards the promised land. Like Israel, those whom God has brought into the Kingdom have received an inheritance.

Elsewhere in the New Testament the language of inheritance occurs repeatedly. Followers of Christ inherit the Kingdom of God (Matthew 25.34), the earth (Matthew 5.5), salvation (Hebrews 1.14), blessing (1 Peter 3.9), glory (Romans 8.17-18), a new heaven and a new earth (Revelation 21.1-7). In all of these instances it is clear that the idea of inheritance, so closely tied to the land in the Old Testament, has been transformed in the light of Christ.

Ephesians 2.11-3.6

This passage contains a clear statement of the radical transformation of the Old Testament promises brought about by Christ. Gentiles were once *strangers to the covenants of promise* (2.21), but now they are *fellow citizens and members of the household of God* (2.19), *fellow heirs, members of the same body, and partakers of the promise.* (3.6). All of this is so because in Christ Jesus they have been brought near (2.13). Again, the promises of God stand; but their meaning and implications have been transformed through their fulfilment in Jesus Christ. Once again, the promise of land has been reinterpreted.

In these and many other passages Paul is simply working out the implications of his assertion that *all the promises of God find their Yes in*

[Christ] (2 Corinthians 1.20). In the light of Christ nothing remains the same, everything is changed.

OLD TESTAMENT PERSPECTIVES IN LIGHT OF NEW TESTAMENT PERSPECTIVES

If we turn again to the five Old Testament perspectives outlines previously, what can we say about them in the light of the New Testament?

Land as Gift

The idea of land as gift is not absent from the New Testament but is placed in a new context. The Old Testament emphasis on the universal sovereignty of God over all lands and nations is reinforced and developed with reference to the universal lordship of Jesus Christ. Thus, on the one hand, the idea of a special piece of land being specially gifted disappears, while on the other the corollary of Christ's lordship is that, ultimately, all land is gift. In other words, all land is gift, but no land is inheritance - no land is specially given to those who stand in relationship with God. The inheritance of the people of God in the New Testament is of a different order.

Land as Task

In many respects land as task has a continuing significance. The ethical demand of the New Testament requires that the people of God work out their way of life - personal, political, social and economic - in the context of the society in which they are placed. The church, too, has an embodied existence. However, the nature of the task does change. It is no longer a task for a particular people in a particular place, given for that purpose. It is, instead, a task for the people of God embodied in the church in all its diversity in all the places where God has established it. It is no longer a matter of living by an all encompassing law given by God to a whole people. It is, instead, a matter of taking the whole body of biblical teaching on life and society and applying it in communities and in places where the lordship of Christ is not acknowledged.

Conseqently, it is no easy matter to work out the meaning and implications of that body of teaching for the societies in which we live. Nevertheless, correctly understood, the Old Testament vision of land as task still has relevance for the people of God in the twenty-first century.

Land as Temptation

The Old Testament warnings against the temptation of land remain relevant. Israel's temptation was to live in the land on its own terms rather than God's. The same temptation faces us.

Of course, what that meant for Israel is different from what it means for us. The temptation for us is to identify our land as the special gift of God, to believe that we can easily transpose the Old Testament's standards for life in the land to our own society, to see our space as holy space. But we share with Israel the temptation to see land as an end in itself, and to believe that our well being and our flourishing is tied up with a particular piece of turf. Israel lost sight of its misson and its calling as a result, and we can do the same.

No matter how central the land to the promise, no matter how great a blessing to the people, possession of the land was never the final purpose of God for Israel. Abraham remained a sojourner in the land of promise, looking forward to the city which has foundations whose builder and maker is God (see Hebrews 11.10).

Like Abraham, New Testament believers also look forward. No matter how precious or important the place where we are from may be, no matter how much it is home for us, those who are in Christ are themselves sojourners who look forward to the heavenly city, the new heavens and the new earth - that is, who look forward to being finally home.

Land as Holy

Ultimately, the land was holy because Israel's holy God made it so by his presence. In the New Testament, however, the presence of God with humanity was found not in a place but in a person - Jesus - and in the community he established. Consequently, there is no holy land, no holy ground, no holy space. While few would claim that their land consititutes such holy ground, there is always the danger that we act as though our land has - somehow - a greater God-given worth than other lands. This is one of our temptations.

But "holy space is where Jesus is; and because as risen Lord he is free to move where he wills, there can be no sacred as opposed to profane territory, no genuine 'holy land'."[6]

Land as Home

If there is a temptation to stay too rooted to the land and to forget that we are sojourners, there is equally a danger that we can spiritualise Christian life to the point where we lose sight of the human need for rootedness and home which is part of God's gift to us.

The New Testament is well aware of the significance of home, of place and of belonging for human existence. When God came among humanity he did so, not in some abstract way, but in a very particular way. He came as a particular Jew born to a particular family, of a particular tribe.

In his words and deeds Jesus recognised the importance of home. For the prodigal son, the strongest need he has in his degredation and misery is for home (Luke 15.18-20). For the demoniac living by the graves his healing is not just physical but involves returning to the place that was once home (Mark 5.19).

When God called men and women to faith he gave them an identity and a place of belonging - they were in Christ and they were in the church. But they were the church in a particular place - Corinth, Antioch, Jerusalem. And the particularities of place shaped them as people and as church.

Nothing in the New Testament undermines the truth that we are made as people who need to be rooted, who need to belong, and who need a place to be home. This is part of God's gift to us. If the land can be a temptation by blinding us to the wider vision of belonging to the church and awaiting the new heavens and the new earth, so we can also be tempted to deny the need for home, the need for rootedness. We can be tempted to condemn those in whom the sense of rootedness is strong, not recognising that in doing so we are condemning people for being the way God has made them and us.

...AND NATION

The land is nothing without a people whose history and life gives it meaning. Similarly, few peoples or nations are able to sustain themselves without at least the aspiration to embody their community in a particular place - Palestinians, Kurds and Armenians all come to mind as national communities whose relationship with their land is problematic, and who seek some kind of fuller embodiment of their communities in ancestral lands.

Israel provides a biblical model of this intimate and mutual relationship between a land and a people and much of what has already been said of land could equally well apply to the nation.

THE PEOPLE OF GOD IN THE OLD TESTAMENT
A Covenanted People

When God made his covenant with Abraham, it included not only the promise of land but the promise of a nation: *I will make you into a great nation and I will bless you* (Genesis 12.1), *Look up at the heavens and count the stars...So shall your offspring be* (Genesis 15.5), *I will establish my covenant as an everlasting covenant between me and you and your descendants, after you for the generations to come, to be your God and the God of your descendants after you* (Genesis 17.7), *I will surely bless you and make your descendants as numerous as the stars in the sky and the sand on the seashore* (Genesis 22.17).

The story of the people of Israel and their relationship to God, established by the covenant, is the constant theme of the Old Testament.

God's commitment to his covenant and, therefore, to his people Israel, runs like a thread through the text (Exodus 6.2-8; Deuteronomy 1.8; 2 Samuel 7.4-17; Isaiah 41.21-23). Israel's tragic failure to live up to the demands of being the covenanted community is the dark shadow that reappears throughout the nation's history (Exodus 32-33; Judges 1-18; 1 Kings 12.28-33; Isaiah 5.8-25; Micah 6.1-16). Yet despite the struggles of Israel to keep the covenant God's faithfulness to his promises offers hope even in the midst of judgement (Isaiah 42.1-9; Jeremiah 32.31-34; Ezekiel 36.24-38; 37.1-28).

A Chosen People

That God chose Israel is the clear message of the Bible (Psalm 33.12; 135.4). The prophet Isaiah, in particular, stressed Israel's status as the chosen or elect nation (Isaiah 42.1; 43.20; 45.4; 65.9,22). As a result of God's choosing them Israel became his 'treasured possession' (Exodus 19.5; Deuteronomy 7.6; 14.2; 26.18). However, against the temptation to assume that Israel was chosen because of some special quality of the nation, the Bible stresses that the reasons for Israel's chosenness have nothing to do with Israel itself. Israel was not chosen because the nation had a greater love for God, nor because they were particularly faithful to God. Instead, they were chosen because of God's love: *The Lord set his affection on your forefathers and loved them, and he chose you, their descendants, above all nations, as it is today* (Deuteronomy 10.15; see also 4.37; 7.7-8). Israel, then, may be a chosen people, but that is not a reason to boast.

A Holy People

The covenant made demands of the people of Israel. Abraham and his descendants were required to keep the covenant, symbolised by submitting to the rite of circumcision (Genesis 17.9-11; see also Genesis 26.5). Later, when the people escaped from Egypt and began the journey towards the promised land, God made a covenant with them at Mount Sinai (Exodus 19.3-9). With the covenant came a complex and comprehensive set of laws to guide all aspects of the life of the people in the land God was going to give them. Obedience to the law

would ensure Israel's well-being (Deuteronomy 28.1-14), while disobedience would bring judgement (28.15-68).

However, at the heart of the law, lay the regulations for the proper
worship of God through which the people maintained their relationship with God and maintained their status as a holy people: *If you obey
me fully and keep my covenant...you will be for me a kingdom of priests and a
holy nation* (Exodus 19.5-6). The rationale for the legal codes of Leviticus is repeatedly expressed in the refrain, *You shall be holy, for I am holy*
(Leviticus 11.44-45; 19.2; 20.7,26). The sanctifying presence of a
holy God demanded a sanctified people; this, not so much for their
own sake, but so that they might be witnesses to the nations of the
holiness of God and of the true nature of human community.

As John Gammie notes, there are different perceptions of the meaning of this demand for holiness throughout the Old Testament: "For
the prophets it was a cleanness of social justice, for the priests a cleanness of proper ritual and maintenance of separation, for the sages it
was a cleanness of inner integrity and individual moral acts."[7] However, what all these ideas have in common is the understanding that
the whole of life must be lived in purity before God.

A Witnessing People

The covenant with Abraham promised not only blessing for Abraham's
descendants but, though them, blessing for the nations: *...all peoples on
earth will be blessed through you* (Genesis 12.3), *...through your offspring all
nations on earth will be blessed because you have obeyed me* (Genesis 22.18; see
also Genesis 18.18; 26.4; 28.14). Indeed, "the ultimate purpose of
Israel's existence is to reveal the greatness of God's name (2 Samuel
7.23; 1 Kings 8.43,60; 1 Chronicles 22.5; 2 Chronicles 6.33; Isaiah
12.4)."[8] The Sinai covenant makes clear that while Israel is special to
God, God remains Lord of all, and the people of Israel are to be
priests, mediators, for the world: *Although the whole earth is mine, you will
be for me a kingdom of priests and a holy nation* (Exodus 19.5-60).

The prophets, in particular, emphasise this universal dimension of
Israel's calling, looking forward to a time when the nations would

recognise the Lordship of God (Isaiah 2.2-4; 66.18-20; Joel 2.8-32). The prophet Isaiah envisages the fulfilment of this aspect of Israel's calling coming about through the work of 'the Servant of the Lord', who will be a light for the Gentiles and will bring justice and salvation to all nations (Isaiah 42.1; 51.4-5; 52.10; 61.1-2).

THE PEOPLE OF GOD BE-TWEEN THE TESTAMENTS[9]
The Nation, Nationalism and the Maccabean Revolt

Israel's failure to keep the covenant resulted in divine punishment, first with the destruction and exile of the northern kingdom of Israel in 722 BC (2 Kings 17.1-23), then with the final fall of Jerusalem and the exile of the southern kingdom of Judah in 586 BC (2 Chronicles 36.15-20). After their return to the land beginning in 538 BC, the people, under the leadership of Ezra and Nehemiah in particular, set about reconstituting the people of Israel in the land of Israel. The Temple was gradually rebuilt and the Passover celebrated once more. Thus Israel's identity as a kingdom of priests was reasserted. The people also committed themselves to be a holy nation through taking action against the practice of intermarriage and the exploitation of the poor.

Israel's tenuous independence did not last long. In 334 BC Alexander the Great began his military campaigns in Asia Minor and Israel soon acknowledged his authority. Following Alexander's death in 323 BC his kingdom was divided among his generals and control of Israel changed hands repeatedly. Eventually, those known as the Seleucids gained the upper hand and Israel came under the rule of Antiochus III (200 BC).

The commitment to Greek culture that was a mark of Alexander's reign and that of some of his successors was problematic for Israel. Greek culture and religion sat uneasily alongside the Jewish people's commitment to their God and to the law. While some Jews accommodated themselves to the new situation, the great majority continued to resist - passively - the encroachment of Greek values. However, another Seleucid king, Antiochus IV, chose to actively pursue a policy of 'hellenisation', with tragic consequences.

The history of this period is extremely complex and many details are still disputed. What is not in dispute is that at one point, probably in 167 BC, Antiochus, believing Israel to be in revolt, sent an army to Jerusalem. As part of his response he attempted to suppress Jewish worship. "This involved the cessation of temple worship, the desecration of things sacred to the Jews, the burning of Torah scrolls, and the propagation of paganism by coercion."[10]

The response to this assault on Israel's religious identity was complex. However, the most notable and effective response was popular revolt, associated with the Hasmonean family and their most outstanding leader Judas 'the Hammer' (Maccabee). In a three year military campaign the Jewish fighters recaptured Jerusalem and purified the Temple once more. Gradually, under the Hasmoneans Israel achieved independence. This was the high point of Jewish religious nationalism, but it was not to last. In 63 BC the Roman general Pompey, responding to appeals from two rivals to the Hasmonean throne, captured Jerusalem.

This was a traumatic time for the Jewish people. "To come once again under foreign domination went against the theological views of many: they were God's chosen people - they were not destined to have Gentiles rule over them."[11] If Israel was to fulfil its calling as a royal priesthood and a holy nation, some kind of survival strategy was required. For some, the only means to maintain the nation's purity was through withdrawal - a course advocated by the Qumran community. For others, the Maccabeans provided the only effective model - armed revolt against foreign overlords. Still others insisted that what was required was an even fiercer commitment to Jewish life and religion - especially in the key areas of the purity laws and Sabbath observance; this was the strategy of the Pharisees.

Despite their differences all were agreed that the people of Israel, the Jewish nation, had to maintain its religious distinctiveness and had to resist anything or anyone which was seen to threaten that distinctiveness. The result was a constant emphasis on the boundaries, a constant judgement concerning who was 'in' and who was 'out'. It was to this people, this nation, that Jesus came.

THE PEOPLE OF GOD AND THE NEW TESTAMENT

Jesus and the Nation

As with the land, the idea of nation was reinterpreted radically by Jesus and his followers. In the New Testament "Jesus appears, not just as the saviour of Israel in fulfilment of prophetic expectation, but also as an embodiment of Israel as they should be."[12] In Matthew's gospel the return of Jesus and his family from Egypt fulfils the words of Hosea: *When Israel was a child, I loved him, out of Egypt I called my son* (Hosea 11.1; see Matthew 2.15).[13] In John's gospel Jesus is identified as the vine (John 15.1-5), an image drawn from the Old Testament where Israel is identified as God's vine or vineyard (Psalm 80.8-16; Isaiah 5.1-7; Jeremiah 2.21). However, the clearest statement of this replacement motif is found in Paul's letter to the Galatian churches.

The promises were spoken to Abraham and to his seed, writes Paul. *The Scripture does not say 'and to seeds' meaning many people, but 'and to your seed', meaning one person, who is Christ* (Galatians 3.16). 'Seed' was generally understood to refer to Abraham's descendants as a collective entity - that is, the people of Israel. However, Paul, like the other New Testament writers, rejected the assertion that simply belonging to the nation of Israel made one a child of Abraham according to the covenant (Romans 9.6-7). The 'seed' to whom the promise was made was primarily Jesus Christ and those who belong to him (Galatians 3.29). A relationship of faith in Christ, argues Paul, links Gentile Christians to Abraham and to God's covenantal promise.

The whole thrust of the New Testament is that God's promise of blessing for the nations has now been fulfilled in Jesus Christ: The Spirit has been poured our on Jew and Gentile alike (Acts 10.44-48); those who once were far away have been brought near (Ephesians 2.11-22); the Gentiles have been grafted onto the Jewish root (Romans 11.17-24).

The opening chapters of Peter's first letter consistently address the churches of Asia Minor in the language that the Old Testament reserved for Israel. So, they are God's elect (1.1-2), theirs is the inheritance (1.4), they are to be holy as God is holy (1.16), they have been redeemed (1.18). Most decisively, they are *a chosen people, a royal priesthood, a holy nation, a people belonging to God* (2.9). This new people of God is a mixed community of Jews and Gentiles - there is no ethnic distinction. As a result the people of God are no longer tied to one particular land or territory.

THE OLD TESTAMENT PERSPECTIVE IN LIGHT OF THE NEW TESTAMENT PERSPECTIVE
A Covenanted People

God has not abandoned or rescinded his covenant. Rather, the covenant with Abraham has been fulfilled in Jesus Christ. The promises of the covenant have come to fruition and the blessings of the covenant have been poured out on those who are the spiritual heirs of Abraham, whether Jew or Gentile, whether in the land of Israel or beyond.

The covenant people of God remain just that - a people, that is, a community. Thus the new covenant does not deny the fundamental human need for community, belonging and identity. It does, however, insist that the community of the covenant transcends the normative human patterns of community.

We need to be careful that we do not draw too great a contrast between old covenant and new for, in truth, the covenant with Abraham was never simply a national covenant, no matter if it came to be understood that way by some within Israel. The covenant with Abraham created a people consecrated to God, but the end of that covenant was the blessing of the nations and the universal recognition of the Lordship of the God of Israel. Thus the idea of a national covenant is always an aberration.

A Chosen People

The new community of God's people is, like Israel, a community that has come to know God's grace. Like Israel, the church has no claim on God. It is not the love or faithfulness of particular people or peoples that makes them worthy of God's grace. It is rather that the church is chosen because of God's love. Consequently, there is no ground for boasting.

The new community does differ from the community of God in the Old Testament in that there is no ethnic or national dimension to God's choosing of his people. While no community with a clear understanding of the New Testament would explicitly claim that any nation stands in the same relation to God as Israel in the Old Testament, there is, nevertheless, an abiding temptation to see the chosenness of Israel as in some sense a metaphor for our national community's relationship with God. So, while we may not be *chosen* by God, the temptation to assume that we are specially *favoured* by God is great. This is a temptation that few national communities have managed to avoid.[14]

A Holy People

As we have seen, Peter took the Levitical command to be holy in imitation of God's holiness and applied it to the church. The same comprehensive vision of what it means to be holy in the Old Testament is clear in the New Testament. No matter about the precise significance of the law for the people of God in the New Testament, the demand is the same. The church in its relationships both internally and with the wider society is obliged to demonstrate the holy character of God in its life.

Like Israel, the temptation that faces the church is to reduce holiness to performance and to focus only on a handful of 'boundary markers'. Along with this temptation is the temptation to turn the demand for holiness into a judgementalism that excludes those who fail to measure up at the boundaries. This is a long way from the holiness of life demanded of the people of God in both the Old and New Testaments.

A Witnessing People

As Israel's holiness of life was intended to be a witness to Israel's God so the holiness of life of the church is intended to be a witness to the unbelieving world. Witness is not just what the church does; the church itself is a witness when its life conforms to the will of God. John's gospel in particular testifies to the powerful witness of the new community as it demonstrates the love of God in its life (John 13.34-35; 17.23). Similarly, 1 Peter stresses the potent effect of holy living in the new community (1 Peter 2.12, 15; 3.8).

Like Israel, the church is not an end in itself. Instead, it witnesses to something beyond itself. "What the church is, in short, is determined by what the church is destined to become. And the church is directed towards the destiny God intends for humankind - participation in the consummated reign of God."[15]

CONCLUSION

As with land so with nation; as with belonging so with identity - there are two dangers that face us. On the one hand, we can become so tied to a particular land or a particular nation that it distorts and corrupts our understanding of the new covenant and the new community of God. On the other hand, we can reduce kingdom and church to abstractions that fail to speak to the God given human need for belonging and identity. As we saw above the church is always the church in a specific place - Rome, Jerusalem, Ephesus and the like. Even when the church is being discussed in a more abstract way it is being discussed in letters written to concrete communities of believers living in particular places.

What is needed is an a sharply focused understanding of church and kingdom that recognises two key truths. First, the gospel throws down a radical challenge to human notions of belonging and identity. Second, the gospel satisfies and fulfils the human desire for belonging and identity through the kingdom and church. At the same time, this understanding has to recognise the complexity and ambiguity of these matters in the context of a promise inaugurated that awaits ultimate fulfilment. In the final chapter we will try to outline what such an understanding might look like.

6

TRINITY, CHURCH, KINGDOM

The Community of God
in Northern Ireland

THE CHURCH BETWEEN HOPE AND DESPAIR

For Christians the ambiguity between the human reality of identity and belonging and the divine reality of the new community and the Kingdom is not merely an abstraction since this ambiguity is embodied in the existence of the church. Similarly, the church is the place where the tension between the reality of the present and the promise of the future is most acutely felt. It is here that the ambiguity and the tension are, if not resolved, confronted. In the church, located in a particular place and often reflecting the identity of the inhabitants of that place, an alternative way is modelled. The church in its day to day life aims to model community where it is placed. As such it anticipates the full expression of place and identity - the covenanted people of God in the new heavens and the new earth - where belonging and identity are not destroyed but are expressed in their God-given and God-honouring fullness.

'Anticipates' is, of course, the key word here. Everyone is well aware of the church's repeated failure to live up to its calling to model and embody God's alternative community. In an abstract sense the church may well be God's new community, but where the abstraction becomes embodied - as it must - in local congregations, those congregations often reflect the identity and belonging - religious, political, ethnic, national - of the wider community in which they are located.

To take only the most obvious example, a congregation that exists in an ethnically homogenous community cannot but reflect that homogeneity in its own community. Or alternatively, a church that exists in an ethnically diverse community is confronted with two possibilities: on the one hand, it can reflect, or even exacerbate difference and suspicion that might exist between different communities; on the other, it can model a harmoniously diverse community in its own community. That is, the church can reinforce destructive patterns of community - and deny its calling - or it can model alternative forms of community and fulfil its calling. Consequently, every form of identity and belonging that is at odds with the biblical vision of true belonging and community stands as a challenge to the church.

Too often the church fails the challenge - whether consciously or unconsciously - demonstrating its unwillingness or inability to confront false and, sometimes, idolatrous, visions of identity and belonging. Yet, in the grace of God, sometimes the church is enabled and empowered to confront society, holding out and embodying a vision that both confirms the human need for identity and belonging while transcending it in the name of ultimate identity and belonging in the community of God and the Kingdom. The failure of the church should come as little surprise to us for, while the church is holy by virtue of the holiness of Christ, it is at the same time a community of fallen but redeemed people. However, instead of focusing on the failures perhaps we would do better to focus our attention on the echoes and the glimmers that challenge and encourage us to see them more fully displayed in the life and witness of the church.

PROTESTANTS AND THE CHURCH

At this point many Protestants and, in particular, many conservative Protestants find themselves in something of a bind. For, if the key to overcoming false and destructive ideas of identity and belonging lies in the church then this would seem to require a reasonably high view of the church. But this is precisely what many conservative Protestants lack; in fact, this is what many of them consciously reject. The reasons for this are fairly straightforward.

First, Protestant views of the church have been formed historically by the reformation debates about authority. The spurious claims to authority and the abuse of that authority by the institutional church of the sixteenth century were at the core of the reformers' challenge to that institution. Thus Protestantism was born of a mistrust of the institutional church and its claims to authority.

Second, Protestantism, and, in particular, conservative Protestantism, located salvation in the personal spiritual encounter between the individual and God, removing it from the mediation of the church, its clergy and its sacramental system. Religious authenticity was found in the direct, unmediated spiritual experience and the institutional structure through which that experience was given expression was derivative and secondary. Consequently, when Protestants talked about the church and the unity of the church they tended to talk about it in abstract terms - irrespective of splits, schisms and the multiplication of denominations, still true believers were spiritually united to all other true believers who, together, comprised the one church.

Third, Protestantism, with its emphasis on personal salvation was easily seduced by the modern enthronement of the individual. Individual salvation was mediated directly by God without reference to any person or institution, and the individual's spiritual development was mediated directly by the Bible as the source of authority.

These latter phenomena are derived from the first. The reformers' critique of the institution's claims to be the mediator of salvation and the source of authority led to a Protestant emphasis on unmediated access to salvation and authority. The church was bypassed and came to have only a functional role - as the place where believers came together to worship, witness and serve. Much of Protestantism "tended to presuppose the spiritual irrelevance of ecclesiastical structures, and to seek alternative, ad hoc, ways of mobilizing the faithful for mission and mutual care. It has therefore been easy...to see only instrumental significance in [the church's] outward order of life, to regard the 'organised church' as a means toward ends to which it remains external."[1]

The consequences of this low view of the church are everywhere: in the rejection of authority, in the constant splits and factions that mark the Protestant tradition and, in particular, the conservative Protestant tradition, in the proliferation of 'ministries' that are often no more than vehicles for the inflated egos of particular individuals, in the historical amnesia that detaches Protestantism from the living faith of generations of fellow Christians, in the take-it-or-leave-it attitude that sees church as an optional extra in the Christian life.

Clearly, given the near absence of any high view of the church among many conservative Protestants, it will be particularly difficult for these communities to manifest the new community of God and bear witness to the Kingdom and, by so doing, challenge, overcome or witness to notions of identity and belonging that are purely human. Conservative Protestants will need to rediscover the high view of the church that was normative among the reformers.[2]

Two of the key areas that will need to be addressed are:

> the relationship between the church as a spiritual entity, and the church as an embodied entity - that is, the question of the church;

> the relationship between Scripture, tradition and church - that is, the question of authority.

A full-scale discussion of these two crucial issues is beyond the scope of this work. However, some general comments are necessary.

The Question of the Church

In the New Testament, the church is primarily a local visible gathering of committed believers. Jesus calls to himself a group of followers who, in turn, take his message throughout Palestine and beyond, founding communities of believers along the way. These new communities are sustained and supported by the writings of Christian leaders. These letters are almost always addressed to a group of local churches in a particular area or to particular churches. Even those letters that are addressed to individuals (1 & 2 Timothy, Titus) are intended to instruct those individuals in their role as leaders in the church. The New Testament also recognises and encourages interdependence and mutual support among these local churches on the grounds of their common faith in Christ.

Alongside this emphasis on the local church, the letters of Paul to the Ephesians and the Colossians introduce the idea of the church as a heavenly and eschatological entity gathered around Christ in which believers participate as they gather in their local churches (Ephesians 3.1-6: Colossians 1.15-20). Thus every earthly assembly is a manifestation of this heavenly assembly. However, asserting the unity of the heavenly entity without living that unity in the earthly manifestation is, from the biblical perspective, theologically incoherent.

Peter O'Brien summarises Paul's teaching on the church thus:

> *Men and women were called into membership of this one church of Christ, the heavenly assembly, through the preaching of the gospel. They were brought into fellowship with God's Son (cf. 1 Cor 1:9), and to speak of their membership of this heavenly gathering assembled around Christ is another way of referring to this new relationship with him. They and other Christians were to assemble in local congregations here on earth, for this was an important way in which their fellowship with Christ was expressed. Further, as they came together with others who were in fellowship with him, so they not only met with each other—they also met with Christ himself who indwelt them corporately and individually.[3]*

The church, then, is fundamental to salvation. The church proclaims the message of salvation and those saved are made part of the church. The church is neither marginal nor optional in the New Testament, nor is it merely a functional entity. The church is the earthly manifestation and sign of that eschatological salvation which is both a present reality and a future hope.

The Question of Authority

The Protestant suspicion of tradition in general has been shaped by the particular suspicion of tradition as it was understood within medieval Catholicism and in post-Reformation Catholicism. Medieval and Tridentine Catholicism were understood to have established tradition as a parallel source of revelation, alongside the Bible, both under the teaching authority of the church. Thus tradition became the basis for the assertion of particular doctrines that the Reformers were questioning and challenging. Tradition, in this sense, was held to undermine the authority of the Bible and to compromise the truth of the gospel.

Unfortunately, the questioning of this particular idea of tradition as an additional source of revelation ultimately led to a rejection of the legitimacy of tradition in any sense. It is only recently that a number of Protestant theologians have begun to reassess the relationship between Scripture, tradition and church,[4] or to make use of the tradition in their theological work.[5]

These theologians and many others are rediscovering the truth that tradition properly understood, far from undermining biblical authority, safeguards both the authority of the Bible and the truth of the gospel. That proper understanding derives from the Bible itself. So, Timothy is ordered to *guard what has been entrusted to your care* (1 Timothy 6.20). And what is it that has been entrusted to him? It is *the faith, the teaching, sound teaching, good teaching* - phrases that occur 22 times in the three letters Paul wrote to Timothy and Titus. Timothy then is to guard a body of teaching - the gospel as he heard it from Scripture, that is, the Old Testament (2 Timothy 3.14-15), from his family (2 Timothy 1.5) and from Paul himself (2 Timothy 1.13). As a guardian of the faith Timothy is to proclaim it (1 Timothy 4.13) and to pass it on (2 Timothy 2.2). Paul himself followed a similar pattern: *I received from the Lord what I also passed on to you* (1 Corinthians 11.23; see also 1 Corinthians 15.3; 2 Thessalonians 2.15).

Tradition, then, was the authoritative understanding of the gospel proclaimed and passed on in the church. The importance of the tradition was clear in the early church's encounters with heretical teachers - many of whom proclaimed their faithfulness to Scripture. Against their false claims leaders in the early church such as Irenaeus and Tertullian asserted that the truth of the gospel had been made known by the apostles to the churches they founded and passed on in the church. The authoritative interpretation of the Bible was only possible within the church which 'knew the story' of God's dealings with humanity and therefore had the key to the understanding of Scripture. The tradition established the boundaries for the reading and interpretation of Scripture and set the boundaries for the true understanding of the gospel.

Tradition, then, is nothing more than 'Scripture rightly understood' and Scripture is rightly understood only in the church. This is not to say that tradition is a fixed set of doctrines and beliefs alongside the Bible. Tradition is dynamic, constantly interacting with Scripture in the church. Tradition is marked by both continuity and change. So, for example, Trinitarian doctrine in the early church developed over a period of time. The tradition - the interpretation of the Bible's revelation of God - developed during that period and, as it developed, the boundaries of what was compatible with the Christian doctrine of God became clearer. "Tradition therefore," writes DH Williams, "is a matter of both *continuity* and *change*, and of development on the basis of the Tradition's past that leads to revision of that past in the present."[6]

COVENANT, KINGDOM AND TRINITY

If Protestants can recover both a high view of the church and a positive assessment of the role of tradition, then they might be in a position to envision a church that by embodying a godly vision offers an alternative to the models of identity and belonging that dominate our society and that have often been so destructive. What might such a church look like?

The Church as the Community of the Covenant

The three synoptic gospels and Paul recount the events of the last supper (Matthew 26.20-35; Mark 12-26; Luke 7-23; 1 Corinthians 11.23-26). Each writer notes that Jesus spoke of the last supper as a covenant and thereby identified his death as a covenant sacrifice. This sacrifice would mark a new covenant between God and God's people, represented by the twelve. Wherever churches were founded the Lord's Supper was observed and those who had been called by God into the church participated in the Lord's Supper as the sign of their own participation in the covenant that God had made with his people through Christ's death.

The implications of this are clear: there is only one valid covenant and only one covenanted community. In a Protestant tradition that has been shaped by covenantal thinking, the temptation to describe political activity in terms of a covenant is one that we have given in to. Of course, this temptation is not uniquely faced by Irish Protestants. Many communities have given in to the temptation to elide the community of the church and the national community, and in doing so they have not always used the motif of covenant as the theological rationale. However, among Protestants in Ireland this covenant motif has been the core means of expressing the relationship between God and the national community.

Such a procedure is illegitimate for a number of reasons. First, while the Bible recognises covenants initiated by human beings, these are always covenants made with other human beings, not with God; divine covenants are always initiated by God. So God is not a party to any covenant that he has not initiated. Second, the whole thrust of the Bible is the anticipation of that everlasting covenant God will make with his people, a covenant that is both "climactic and eternal,"[7] a covenant that was ratified in the death of Jesus. Third, the community with whom God enters into relationship through the covenant is clearly identified - it is those who are believers in Jesus Christ.

This clear and consistent biblical teaching has obvious implications for the Ulster Covenant discussed earlier. This covenant was, in reality no covenant except inasmuch as the people who signed it were making a covenant - in the sense of a solemn promise - with one another. The Ulster Covenant, therefore, has no spiritual significance whatsoever - positive or negative. God was not a party to the Ulster Covenant.

The Church as the Sign of the Kingdom

While the church is a major theme of the New Testament, it plays little direct part in Jesus' own teaching. Instead, at the centre of Jesus' teaching was the kingdom of God (Mark 1.15). This then raises the question of how the church relates to the kingdom. On the one hand there has been a tendency to see the two as synonymous - the church is the manifestation of the kingdom in the world. On the other hand there has been a tendency to emphasise the kingdom at the expense of the church especially among those who find themselves frustrated with the failings of the church. Neither of these is valid. Instead, the church has to be seen in the context of and in relation to the kingdom.

The literature on the kingdom is immense and ever expanding. Again, this is not the place to delve into the theology of the kingdom. However, it is appropriate at this point to try to summarise the nature of the kingdom that Jesus proclaimed. Stanley Grenz offers the following summary:

> *The kingdom of God comes as that order of peace, righteousness, justice, and love that God gives to the world. This gift arrives in an ultimate way only at the eschaton, at the renewal of the world brought by Jesus' return. Nevertheless, the power of the kingdom is already at work, for it breaks into the present from the future. As a result, we can experience the divine reign in a partial, yet real sense prior to the great eschatological day.*[8]

We need only add that the power of the kingdom at work is seen in the words and works of Jesus Christ.

How, then, does the church relate to the kingdom? First, the church is the product of the proclamation of the kingdom. Men and women are challenged to submit to the kingly rule of God. In doing so they become part of the community of God - the church. That community in turn is tasked with proclaiming the kingly rule of God to others in its words and works.

The church, then, in its life and ministry is to be a sign of the kingdom of God. In other words, in its life together the Christian community should provide a model of what it means to be a community living under the rule of God. The church should be the place where that peace, righteousness, justice and love that will one day be fully known are demonstrated. Consequently, if the proclamation of the rule of God is not accompanied by its embodiment in the life of the community - the church - then its proclamation is rendered ineffective.

Again, the implications of this are clear: if churches in Northern Ireland fail to demonstrate in their own life the values of the kingdom of God, their words become ineffectual. To the extent that churches in Northern Ireland have simply absorbed and replicated the values of the kingdoms of this world, they have undermined the very gospel they proclaim.

The Church as the Trinitarian Community

The Christian community is the work of God - Father, Son and Holy Spirit. The whole of the New Testament reflects the work of the Trinity in creating and sustaining the church and the Trinitarian orientation of the church's ministry and worship.[9]

The Christian community should also be the place where the life of God is made known. This means that the church above all should be that "ikon of the Triunity" of which Ware speaks.[10] As the divine community of Father, Son and Holy Spirit is marked by mutual love, so should the church. This after all, is the message of John's gospel:

> *My prayer is not for them alone. I pray also for those who will believe in me through their message, that all of them may be one, Father, just as you are in me and I am in you. May they also be in us so that the world may believe that you have sent me. I have given them the glory that you gave me, that they may be one as we are one: I in them and you in me. May they be brought to complete unity to let the world know that you sent me and have loved them even as you have loved me* (John 17.20-23).

Crucially, this prayer of Jesus links the church's manifestation of the life of God with the church's witness to Jesus Christ. The message must be proclaimed, but the power of that word is profoundly determined by the power of the church's life together in the image of God. In a similar vein Peter reminds Christians that the work of God in their lives has as its end that they might *participate in the divine nature* (2 Peter 1.4). While the precise meaning of this term is open to interpretation, the broad significance of it is indisputable. Since the goal of the Christian life is to be conformed to the divine life that transformation should be taking place in the here and now. So, Peter immediately encourages those he is writing to as people of faith to add to that faith. Their lives should be marked by *goodness, knowledge, self-control, perseverance, godliness, brotherly kindness and love* (2 Peter 1.5-7).

Much ink has been spilt on the subject of the marks of the true church. For the Catholic tradition the Nicene Creed's description of the church as one, holy, catholic and apostolic is normative. In the Reformed tradition the emphasis has been on the true preaching of the word, the right administration of the sacraments and the administering of discipline. Yet perhaps it is time to insist that, important as all these characteristics are, the true mark of the church is that it is a body of people who reflect in their own community life the life of the triune God – Father, Son and Holy Spirit.

WHERE DO WE GO FROM HERE?

The challenge to the churches in Northern Ireland is great, but it is also very simple. We should beware of the danger of over complicating matters and, as a result, rendering ourselves unable to respond. Part of the challenge is to recognise the extent to which our values and attitudes are fixed by the society of which we are a part. Our ideas of community and place are determined by the national community of which we are a part and by the land in which we live more than they are by the community of the church.

And why should we be surprised that this is so? We interact with this community and this place every day of our lives. We learn the history of our land and nation, we learn its songs, we recognise its symbols. We hear its stories of triumph, defeat, sorrow and joy told and retold and we tell and retell them to others.

We are not neutral observers of this community or this place. We are participants, we belong and we are what we are by virtue of our participation. Contrast this immersion in this community and this place with our much more limited immersion in the church - that is, beyond the merely functional view of church. It is no wonder that it is so often the power of community and place that determines our understanding of church. This, of course, is about as wrong as it is possible to be.

Consequently, if we are ever going to make any impact on this community, to call it away from its blinkered fixation on passing and transient allegiances, we have to start with ourselves as the people of God. **Doing** church is not enough, we have to learn what it means to **be** church. For if we cannot be church in our community then our words - such as they are - will be of little effect.

It is time to turn away from our activism; time to stop asking, But what can we do? Before we can even begin to address this question we must address the question, What should we be? When we begin to answer this latter question, then the answer to the former question will become clearer.

NOTES

NOTES TO CHAPTER 1

1 See John Guy, *Tudor England* (Oxford: OUP 1990); Diarmaid MacCulloch, *Thomas Cranmer: A Life* (Newhaven and London: Yale UP 1997) *Tudor Church Militant* (London: Allen Lane The Penguin Press 2000)

2 Guy, *Tudor England* p 247

3 Guy, *Tudor England* p 304

4 Guy, *Tudor England* p 277

5 Guy, *Tudor England* p 299

6 See Mark Kishlansky, *A Monarchy Transformed: Britain 1603-1714* (London: Penguin 1997)

7 Kishlansky, *A Monarchy Transformed* p 283

8 Kishlansky, *A Monarchy Transformed* p 265

9 For an analysis of the consolidation of the revolution see Tony Claydon, *William III and the Godly Commonwealth* (Cambridge: CUP 1996)

10 Kishlansky, *A Monarchy Transformed* p 251

11 Kishlansky, *A Monarchy Transformed* p 252

12 See Linda Colley, *Britons: Forging the Nation 1707-1837* (London: Vintage 1996); JCD Clark *English Society 1660-1832* (Cambridge: CUP 2000)

13 Colley, *Britons* p 52

14 Colley, *Britons* p 3

15 Paul Langford, 'The Eighteenth Century' pp 399-469 in Kenneth O Morgan (ed.), *The Oxford History of Britain* (Oxford: OUP 1988) p 450

16 Colley, *Britons* p 19

17 Colley, *Britons* p 20

18 Colley, *Britons* p 23

19 See John Wolffe, *God and Greater Britain: Religion and National Life in Britain and Ireland 1843-1945* (London: Routledge 1994); *The Protestant Crusade in Great Britain 1829-60* (Oxford: OUP 1991)

20 See Brian Stanley, *The Bible and the Flag: Protestant Missions and British Imperialism in the Nineteenth and Twentieth Centuries* (Leicester: Apollos 1990)

21 Wolffe, *God and Greater Britain* p 222

22 cited in Wolffe, *God and Greater Britain* p 222

23 Colley, *Britons* p 349-350

24 cited in Edward Norman, *Anti-Catholicism in Victorian England* (London: Allen and Unwin 1968) p 159-161

25 See David Bebbington, *Evangelicalism in Modern Britain: A History from the 1730s to the 1980s* (Grand Rapids: Baker 1992) pp 1-180; Wolffe, *Protestant Crusade*

26 HCG Matthew, 'The Liberal Age 1815-1914' pp 518-581 in Morgan, (ed.) *The Oxford History* p 555

NOTES TO CHAPTER 2

1 Alvin Jackson, *Ireland 1798-1998* (Oxford: Blackwell 1999) p 57

2 Adrian Hastings, 'Catholic History from Vatican I to John Paul II' pp 1-13 in Adrian Hastings, (ed.) *Modern Catholicism: Vatican II and After* (London: SPCK 1991) p 2

3 Jonathan Bardon, *A History of Ulster* (Belfast: Blackstaff 1992) p 344

4 See RFG Holmes, *Henry Cooke* (Belfast: Christian Journals 1981)

5 See Stewart J Brown, 'Presbyterian Communities, Transatlantic Visions and the Ulster Revival of 1859' pp 87-108 in James Mackey (ed.), *The Cultures of Europe: The Irish Contribution* (Belfast: Institute of Irish Studies 1994) pp 87-108

6 David Hempton and Myrtle Hill, *Evangelical Protestantism in Ulster Society 1740-1890* (London: Routledge 1992) p 146

7 Brown, 'Presbyterian Communities' p 93

8 Brown, 'Presbyterian Communities' p 97

9 See ATQ Stewart, *The Ulster Crisis: Resistance to Home Rule 1912-1914* (Belfast: Blackstaff 1997)

10 *Christian Advocate* 8 January 1886 cited in Hempton and Hill, *Evangelical Protestantism* p 175

11 cited in Jonathan Bardon, *A History of Ulster* (Belfast: Blackstaff 1992) p 437

12 Former Presbyterian moderator Rev Samuel Prenter cited in Thomas Hennessey, *Dividing Ireland: World War 1 and Partition* (London: Routledge 1998) p 18

13 William Moore MP cited in Hennessey, *Dividing Ireland* p 10

14 Andrew Horner MP cited in Hennessey, *Dividing Ireland* p 12

15 Belfast industrialist Frank Johnston cited in Gordon Lucy, *The Great Convention: The Ulster Unionist Convention of 1892* (Lurgan: Ulster Society 1995) p 31

16 *Newsletter* 19 September 1912 cited in Hennessey, *Dividing Ireland* p 16

17 cited in Paul Bew, *Ideology and the Irish Question: Ulster Unionism and Irish Nationalism 1912-1916* (Oxford: OUP 1994) p 29

18 cited in Bew, *Ideology* p 27

19 See Graham Walker, 'Thomas Sinclair: Presbyterian Liberal Unionist' pp 19-40 in Richard English and Graham Walker (eds), *Unionism in Modern Ireland: New Perspectives on Politics and Culture* (Dublin: Gill & Macmillan 1996)

20 Walker, 'Thomas Sinclair' p 32

NOTES TO CHAPTER 3

1 John Whyte, *Interpreting Northern Ireland* (Oxford: Clarendon Press 1990)

2 Whyte, *Interpreting* p 50

3 Whyte, *Interpreting* p 103

4 Whyte, *Interpreting* p 110

5 Whyte, *Interpreting* p 109

6 Whyte, *Interpreting Northern Ireland* p 109

7 John McGarry and Brendan O'Leary, *Explaining Northern Ireland* (Oxford: Blackwell 1995)

8 McGarry and O'Leary, *Explaining* p 213

9 McGarry and O'Leary, *Explaining* p 172

10 McGarry and O'Leary, *Explaining* p 213

11 McGarry and O'Leary, *Explaining* p 212

12 See McGarry and O'Leary, *Explaining* pp 195-196

13 McGarry and O'Leary, *Explaining* p 194

14 McGarry and O'Leary, *Explaining* p 195

15 McGarry and O'Leary, *Explaining* p 197

16 See Steve Bruce, *God Save Ulster: The Religion and Politics of Paisleyism* (Oxford: OUP 1986); *The Red Hand: Protestant Paramilitaries in Northern Ireland* (Oxford: OUP 1992); *The Edge of the Union: The Ulster Loyalist Political Vision* (Oxford: OUP 1994)

17 Bruce, *Edge of the Union* p 2

18 There is both a distinction and a relationship between conservative Protestantism on the one hand and evangelicalism on the other. While many evangelicals would describe themselves as conservative Protestants, there are groups holding to conservative Protestant beliefs that may not necessarily use the label evangelical. Within the Presbyterian tradition and within Anglicanism, for example, there can be a preference for self-identification with reference to these particular confessional traditions. However, these Christians would have many beliefs and values in common with those who might be more likely to use the label evangelical. Consequently, 'conservative Protestant' is a broader term than 'evangelical' even though there is significant overlap between the two. Where authors being cited use the term evangelical I have used that term. Elsewhere, in this and subsequent chapters, I have chosen to use the term conservative Protestant.

19 Bruce, *Edge of the Union* p 26

20 Bruce, *Edge of the Union* p 25

21 Bruce, *Edge of the Union* p 29-30

22 Donald Harman Akenson, *God's Peoples: Covenant and Land in South Africa, Israel and Ulster* (Ithaca, NY: Cornell University Press 1992)

23 Akenson, *God's Peoples* p 4

24 Akenson, *God's Peoples* p 42

25 Akenson, *God's Peoples* 145

26 See Akenson, *God's Peoples* pp 263-310

27 Akenson, *God's Peoples* p 287

28 Akenson, *God's Peoples* p 294

29 On evangelical attitudes to a broad range of issues in Northern Ireland see Glenn Jordan, *Not of this World? The Evangelical Protestants of Northern Ireland* (Belfast: Blackstaff Press/CCCI 2000)

30 www.dup.org.uk

31 www.ukup.org/home.htm

32 *News Letter* 24 April 1998

33 *News Letter* 21 May 1998

34 See especially Tony Claydon and Ian McBride, 'The Trials of the Chosen People: Recent Interpretations of Protestantism and National Identity in Britain

and Ireland' pp 3-29 in Tony Claydon & Ian McBride (eds), *Protestantism and National Identity* (Cambridge: Cambridge University Press 1998)

35 See Christian Smith, *American Evangelicalism: Embattled and Thriving* (Chicago: University of Chicago Press 1998) especially pp 120-153 and Donald E Miller, *Reinventing American Protestantism: Christianity in the New Millennium* (Berkeley, CA: University of California Press 1999)

36 See especially R. Scott Appleby, *The Ambivalence of the Sacred: Religion, Violence, and Reconciliation* (Lanham, MD: Rowman and Littlefield 1999)

37 Two recently published works that take seriously the religious dimension of the conflict in Ireland are Joseph Liechty and Cecilia Clegg, *Moving Beyond Sectarianism: Religion, Conflict and Reconciliation in Northern Ireland* (Dublin: The Columba Press 2001) and Marcuss Tanner, *Ireland's Holy Wars: The Struggle for a Nation's Soul 1500-2000* (New Haven: Yale University Press 2001)

NOTES TO CHAPTER 4

1 David Nicholls, *Deity and Domination: Images of God and State in the Nineteenth and Twentieth Centuries* London: Routledge 1994) p 2. See also David Nicholls, *God and Government in an Age of Reason* (London: Routledge 1995).

2 See Daniel Block, *The Gods of the Nations* (Leicester: Apollos 2000²)

3 James Dunn, *The Partings of the Ways Between Christianity and Judaism and their Significance for the Character of Christianity* (SCM: London 1991) p 31

4 A recent restatement of this doctrine from an evangelical perspective can be found in David Peterson, *Where Wrath and Mercy Meet* (Carlisle: Paternoster 2001). A critical analysis from an evangelical persepctive can be found in Joel B Green and Mark D Baker, *Recovering the Scandal of the Cross: Atonement in New Testament and Contemporary Contexts* (Downers Grove, IL: IVP 2000).

5 Mark Noll, 'Evangelicalism at its Best' pp 1-26 in Mark Noll and Ronald Thiemann (eds), *Where Shall My Wond'ring Soul Begin? The Landscape of Evangelical Piety and Thought* (Grand Rapids: Eerdmans 2000) p 9

6 Examples include Isaac Watts, *Join All the Glorious Names*; Charles Wesley, '*Tis Finished! the Messiah Dies;* Horatius Bonar, *Here, O My Lord.*

7 See Timothy Gorringe, *God's Just Vengeance* (Cambridge: CUP 1996) pp 156-219

8 William Hutchison and Hartmut Lehmann (eds), *Many are Chosen: Divine Election and Western Nationalism* (Minneapolis: Fortress 1994)

9 Akenson, *God's Peoples*

10 Donald G Bloesch, *God the Almighty: Power, Wisdom, Holiness, Love* (Carlisle: Paternoster 1995) p166

11 Colin Gunton, *The Promise of Trinitarian Theology* (Edinburgh: T&T Clark 1997²) pp3-5 Nor is this simply an evangelical or Protestant problem. As Catholic theologian Karl Rahner notes: "Despite the orthodox confessions of the trinity, Christians are, in their practical life, almost mere 'monotheists'...It is as though this mystery has been revealed for its own sake, and that even after it has been made known to us, it remains, as a reality, locked up within itself. We make statements about it, but as a reality it has nothing to do with us at all." Cited in David S Cunningham *These Three are One: The Practice of Trinitarian Theology* (Oxford: Blackwell 1999) p 29

12 Augustine, *Confessions* 13.1; *Trinity* 9.2-8; 14.11-12

13 Kallistos Ware, *The Orthodox Way* (Crestwood, NY: St Valdimir's Seminary Press 1998²) p 27

14 Stanley Grenz, *Theology for the Community of God* (Carlisle: Paternoster 1994) p 88

15 Genesis 1.26-27; 5.1-3; 9.6

16 Colin Gunton, *Christ and Creation* (Carlisle: Paternoster 1992) p 101

17 Cunningham, *These Three are One* p 171

18 Cunningham, *These Three are One* p 171

19 Ware, *The Orthodox Way* 38-39

NOTES TO CHAPTER 5

1 See Pico Iyer, *The Global Soul: Jet Lag, Shopping Malls and the Search for Home* (London: Bloomsbury 2000)

2 Simon Schama, *Landscape and Memory* (London: Fontana Press 1996) p 15

3 For some of the following categories see Walter Brueggemann, *The Land* (Philadelphia: Fortress Press 1977) pp 45-70

4 Walter Brueggemann, *The Covenanted Self: Explorations in Law and Covenant* (Minneapolis: Fortress Press 1999) p 100

5 See Peter Walker, 'The Land in the Apostles' Writings' pp 81-99 and 'The Land and Jesus Himself' pp 100-120 in Philip Johnston and Peter Walker (eds), *The Land of Promise: Biblical, Theological and Contemporary Perspectives* (Leicester: Apollos 2000)

6 Dale C Allison Jnr, 'Land' pp 642-644 in Ralph P Martin and H Peter Davids (eds), *The Dictionary of the Later New Testament and its Developments* (Leicester: IVP 1997) p 644

7 John G Gammie, *Holiness in Israel* (Minneapolis: Fortress Press 1989) p 196

8 Andreas Kostenberger, 'Nations' pp 676-678 in Desmond Alexander & Brian Rosner (eds), *New Dictionary of Biblical Theology* (Leicester: IVP 2000) p 677

9 On the history of the period see Lester L Grabbe, *An Introduction to First Century Judaism: Jewish Religion and History in the Second Temple Period* (Edinburgh: T&T Clark 1996). On the religious groups and revolutionary movements see Richard Horsley with John S Hanson, *Bandits, Prophets and Messiahs: Popular Movements at the Time of Jesus* (New York: Harper & Row 1985) and Anthony Saldarini, *Pharisees, Scribes and Sadducees in Palestinian Society* (Edinburgh: T&T Clark 1989)

10 Horsley and Hanson, *Bandits, Prophets and Messiahs* p 17

11 Grabbe, *Introduction* p 14

12 Steve Motyer, 'Israel (Nation)' pp 581-587 in Alexander & Rosner *NDBT* p 584

13 See Dale C Allison, 'The Son of God as Israel: A Note on Matthean Christology' pp 74-81 in *Irish Biblical Studies* 9 (1987)

14 See, for example, Akenson, *God's Peoples*; Conrad Cherry, *God's New Israel: Religious Interpretations of American Destiny* (Englewood Cliffs, NJ: Prentice-Hall 1972); Dorian Llywelyn, *Sacred Place, Chosen People* (Cardiff: University of Wales Press 1999); Hutchison and Lehmann, *Many are Chosen*

15 Grenz, *Theology* p 623

NOTES TO CHAPTER 6

1 David S Yeago, 'The Church as Polity? The Lutheran Context of Robert W Jenson's Ecclesiology' pp 201-237 in Colin E Gunton (ed.) *Trinity, Time, and Church: A Response to the Theology of Robert W. Jenson* (Grand Rapids: Eerdmans 2000) p 210

2 See John Calvin, *Institutes* 4.1.4; Martin Luther: "The Christian Church is your mother who gives birth to you through the Word" Martin Luther, *Works* 51 p166

3 Peter T. O'Brien, 'Church' pp123-131 in Gerald F Hawthorne, Ralph P Martin and Daniel G Reid (eds), *Dictionary of Paul and His Letters* (Leicester: IVP 1993) p 126

4 See, for example, Alister McGrath, 'Engaging the Great Tradition: Evangelical Theology and the Role of Tradition' pp 139-158 in John G Stackhouse Jr. (ed.) *Evangelical Futures: A Conversation on Theological Method* (Leicester: Apollos 2000) and especially DH Williams, *Retrieving the Tradition and Renewing Evangelicalism: A Primer for Suspicious Protestants* (Grand Rapids: Eerdmans 1999)

5 See, for example, Thomas Oden, *Systematic Theology* (3 vols) (San Francisco: Harper & Row 1987-1992) and Robert Webber, *Ancient-Future Faith: Rethinking Evangelicalism for a Postmodern World* (Grand Rapids: Baker 1999].

6 Williams, *Retrieving the Tradition* p 38

7 Paul Williamson 'Covenant' pp 419-429 in Alexander & Rosner *NDBT* p 427

8 Grenz, *Theology* p 620

9 See Boris Bobrinskoy, *The Mystery of the Trinity: Trinitarian Experience and Vision in the Biblical and Patristic Tradition* (**Crestwood,NY: SVS Press 1999**) pp 100-139

10 Ware, *The Orthodox Way* p 39

BIBLIOGRAPHY

Akenson, Donald Harman, *God's Peoples: Covenant and Land in South Africa, Israel and Ulster* (Ithaca, NY: Cornell University Press 1992)

Alexander, Desmond & Rosner, Brian (eds), *New Dictionary of Biblical Theology* (Leicester: IVP 2000)

Allison, Dale C, 'The Son of God as Israel: A Note on Matthean Christology' pp 74-81 in *Irish Biblical Studies* 9 (1987)

Appleby, R. Scott, *The Ambivalence of the Sacred: Religion, Violence, and Reconciliation* (Lanham, MD: Rowman and Littlefield 1999)

Bardon, Jonathan *A History of Ulster* (Belfast: Blackstaff 1992)

Bebbington, David, *Evangelicalism in Modern Britain: A History from the 1730s to the 1980s* (Grand Rapids: Baker 1992)

Bew, Paul, *Ideology and the Irish Question: Ulster Unionism and Irish Nationalism 1912-1916* (Oxford: OUP 1994)

Block, Daniel, *The Gods of the Nations* (Leicester: Apollos 2000²)

Bloesch, Donald G, *God the Almighty: Power, Wisdom, Holiness, Love* (Carlisle: Paternoster 1995)

Bobrinskoy, Boris, *The Mystery of the Trinity: Trinitarian Experience and Vision in the Biblical and Patristic Tradition* (Crestwood,NY: SVS Press 1999)

Brown, Stewart J, 'Presbyterian Communities, Transatlantic Visions and the Ulster Revival of 1859' pp 87-108 in Mackey, *The Cultures of Europe*

Bruce, Steve, *God Save Ulster: The Religion and Politics of Paisleyism* (Oxford: OUP 1986)

> *The Red Hand: Protestant Paramilitaries in Northern Ireland* (Oxford: OUP 1992)

> *The Edge of the Union: The Ulster Loyalist Political Vision* (Oxford: OUP 1994)

Brueggemann, Walter, *The Land* (Philadelphia: Fortress Press 1977)

> *The Covenanted Self: Explorations in Law and Covenant* (Minneapolis: Fortress Press 1999)

Cherry, Conrad, *God's New Israel: Religious Interpretations of American Destiny* (Englewood Cliffs, NJ: Prentice-Hall 1972)

Clark, JCD *English Society 1660-1832* (Cambridge: CUP 2000)

Claydon, Tony, *William III and the Godly Commonwealth* (Cambridge: CUP 1996)

Claydon, Tony and McBride, Ian, 'The Trials of the Chosen People: Recent Interpretations of Protestantism and National Identity in Britain and Ireland' pp 3-29 in Claydon & McBride, *Protestantism and National Identity*

Claydon, Tony and McBride, Ian (eds), *Protestantism and National Identity* (Cambridge: Cambridge University Press 1998)

Colley, Linda, *Britons: Forging the Nation 1707-1837* (London: Vintage 1996)

Cunningham, David S, *These Three are One: The Practice of Trinitarian Theology* (Oxford: Blackwell 1999)

Dunn, James, *The Partings of the Ways Between Christianity and Judaism and their Significance for the Character of Christianity* (SCM: London 1991)

English, Richard & Walker, Graham (eds), *Unionism in Modern Ireland: New Perspectives on Politics and Culture* (Dublin: Gill & Macmillan 1996)

Gammie, John G, *Holiness in Israel* (Minneapolis: Fortress Press 1989)

Gorringe, Timothy, *God's Just Vengeance* (Cambridge: CUP 1996)

Grabbe, Lester L, *An Introduction to First Century Judaism: Jewish Religion and History in the Second Temple Period* (Edinburgh: T&T Clark 1996)

Green, Joel B and Baker, Mark D, *Recovering the Scandal of the Cross: Atonement in New Testament and Contemporary Contexts* (Downers Grove, IL: IVP 2000)

Grenz, Stanley, *Theology for the Community of God* (Carlisle: Paternoster 1994)

Gunton, Colin, *Christ and Creation* (Carlisle: Paternoster 1992)

   The Promise of Trinitarian Theology (Edinburgh: T&T Clark 1997[2])

Gunton, Colin E (ed.), *Trinity, Time, and Church: A Response to the Theology of Robert W. Jenson* (Grand Rapids: Eerdmans 2000)

Guy, John, *Tudor England* (Oxford: OUP 1990)

Hawthorne, Gerald F, Martin, Ralph P and Reid, Daniel G (eds), *Dictionary of Paul and His Letters* (Leicester: IVP 1993)

Hastings, Adrian, 'Catholic History from Vatican I to John Paul II' pp 1-13 in Hastings, *Modern Catholicism*

Hastings, Adrian (ed.), *Modern Catholicism: Vatican II and After* (London: SPCK 1991)

Hempton, David and Hill, Myrtle, *Evangelical Protestantism in Ulster Society 1740-1890* (London: Routledge 1992)

Hennessey, Thomas, *Dividing Ireland: World War 1 and Partition* (London: Routledge 1998)

Holmes, RFG, *Henry Cooke* (Belfast: Christian Journals 1981)

Horsley, Richard with Hanson, John S, *Bandits, Prophets and Messiahs: Popular Movements at the Time of Jesus* (New York: Harper & Row 1985)

Hutchison, William and Lehmann, Hartmut (eds), *Many are Chosen: Divine Election and Western Nationalism* (Minneapolis: Fortress 1994)

Iyer, Pico, *The Global Soul: Jet Lag, Shopping Malls and the Search for Home* (London: Bloomsbury 2000)

Jackson, Alvin, *Ireland 1798-1998* (Oxford: Blackwell 1999)

Johnston, Philip and Walker, Peter (eds), *The Land of Promise: Biblical, Theological and Contemporary Perspectives* (Leicester: Apollos 2000)

Jordan, Glenn, *Not of this World? The Evangelical Protestants of Northern Ireland* (Belfast: Blackstaff Press/CCCI 2000)

Kishlansky, Mark, *A Monarchy Transformed: Britain 1603-1714* (London: Penguin 1997)

Langford, Paul, 'The Eighteenth Century' pp 399-469 in Morgan, *The Oxford History of Britain*

Liechty, Joseph and Clegg, Cecilia, *Moving Beyond Sectarianism: Religion, Conflict and Reconciliation in Northern Ireland* (Dublin: The Columba Press 2001)

Llywelyn, Dorian, *Sacred Place, Chosen People* (Cardiff: University of Wales Press 1999)

Lucy, Gordon, *The Great Convention: The Ulster Unionist Convention of 1892* (Lurgan: Ulster Society 1995)

MacCulloch, Diarmaid, *Thomas Cranmer: A Life* (Newhaven and London: Yale University Press 1997)

Tudor Church Militant (London: Allen Lane The Penguin Press 2000)

Mackey, James (ed.), *The Cultures of Europe: The Irish Contribution* (Belfast: Institute of Irish Studies 1994)

Martin, Ralph P and Davids, H Peter (eds), *The Dictionary of the Later New Testament and its Developments* (Leicester: IVP 1997)

Matthew, HCG, 'The Liberal Age 1815-1914' pp 518-581 in Morgan, *The Oxford History of Britain*

McGarry, John and O'Leary, Brendan, *Explaining Northern Ireland* (Oxford: Blackwell 1995)

McGrath, Alister, 'Engaging the Great Tradition: Evangelical Theology and the Role of Tradition' pp 139-158 in Stackhouse, *Evangelical Futures*

Miller, Donald E, *Reinventing American Protestantism: Christianity in the New Millennium* (Berkeley, CA: University of California Press 1999)

Morgan, Kenneth O (ed.), *The Oxford History of Britain* (Oxford: OUP 1988)

Nicholls, David, *Deity and Domination: Images of God and State in the Nineteenth and Twentieth Centuries* London: Routledge 1994)

God and Government in an Age of Reason (London: Routledge 1995)

Noll, Mark, 'Evangelicalism at its Best' pp 1-26 in Noll & Thiemann, *Where Shall My Wond'ring Sould Begin?*

Noll, Mark and Thiemann, Ronald (eds), *Where Shall My Wond'ring Sould Begin? The Landscape of Evangelical Piety and Thought* (Grand Rapids: Eerdmans 2000)

Norman, Edward, *Anti-Catholicism in Victorian England* (London: Allen and Unwin 1968)

Oden, Thomas, *Systematic Theology* (3 vols) (San Francisco: Harper & Row 1987-1992)

Peterson, David, *Where Wrath and Mercy Meet* (Carlisle: Paternoster 2001)

Saldarini, Anthony, *Pharisees, Scribes and Sadducees in Palestinian Society* (Edinburgh: T&T Clark 1989)

Schama, Simon, *Landscape and Memory*(London: Fontana Press 1996)

Smith, Christian, *American Evangelicalism: Embattled and Thriving* (Chicago: University of Chicago Press 1998)

Stackhouse Jr., John G (ed.), *Evangelical Futures: A Conversation on Theological Method* (Leicester: Apollos 2000)

Stanley, Brian, *The Bible and the Flag:Protestant Missions and British Imperialism in the Nineteenth and Twentieth Centuries* (Leicester: Apollos 1990)

Stewart, ATQ, *The Ulster Crisis: Resistance to Home Rule 1912-1914* (Belfast: lackstaff 1997)

Tanner, Marcuss , *Ireland's Holy Wars: The Struggle for a Nation's Soul 1500-2000* (New Haven: Yale University Press 2001)

Walker, Graham, 'Thomas Sinclair: Presbyterian Liberal Unionist' pp 19-40 in English & Walker, *Unionism in Modern Ireland*

Walker, Peter, 'The Land in the Apostles' Writings' pp 81-99 and 'The Land and Jesus Himself' pp 100-120 in Johnston & Walker, *The Land of Promise*

Ware, Kallistos, *The Orthodox Way* (Crestwood, NY: St Valdimir's Seminary Press 1998²)

Webber, Robert, *Ancient-Future Faith: Rethinking Evangelicalism for a Postmodern World* (Grand Rapids: Baker 1999].

Whyte, John, *Interpreting Northern Ireland* (Oxford: Clarendon Press 1990)

Williams, DH, *Retrieving the Tradition and Renewing Evangelicalism: A Primer for Suspicious Protestants* (Grand Rapids: Eerdmans 1999)

Wolffe, John, *God and Greater Britain: Religion and National Life in Britain and Ireland 1843-1945* (London: Routledge 1994)

he Protestant Crusade in Great Britain 1829-60 (Oxford: OUP 1991)

Yeago, David S, 'The Church as Polity? The Lutheran Context of Robert W Jenson's Ecclesiology' pp 201-237 in Gunton, *Trinity, Time, and Church*